A CITIZEN'S GUIDE TO DEFICITS AND DEBT

America is currently involved in one of the worst economic crises of modern times. As alarm increases over how the government will balance the budget, handle the debt, and maintain prosperity for the future, the minutia of debts and deficits remains incomprehensible to many. Why is it so hard to find ways to resolve the fiscal crisis? This brief and intelligible book is a guide to understanding both the difficulties involved in managing the federal budget and why the on-going fiscal crisis is so significant for America's future.

In order to introduce the reader to the basic composition of federal spending and to the ways that the government raises revenue, Hudson begins his guide with a "map" clarifying how to navigate the federal budget. He defines basic financial vocabulary and outlines concepts by using clear charts and diagrams that both provide basis for discussion and illustrate key points. With this budget map in mind, the second part of the book lays out how the partisan divide in America helps explain the fiscal crisis. Hudson analyzes the debate on the extent of the fiscal crisis, the ways that political parties have tried to solve it, and the political events and institutions that have surrounded the crisis.

This citizen's guide reveals how differing views of America inform the arguments over deficits and debt. By the time readers finish the book, they will understand that the conflict over deficits and debt is not simply about where to cut or add spending, but instead is a struggle over national priorities and visions for the future.

William E. Hudson is professor of political science at Providence College. He is the author of *American Democracy in Peril 7th ed.*, *The Libertarian Illusion* and *Experiencing Citizenship: Concepts and Models for Service-Learning in Political Science* (with Richard Battistoni). Hudson has published numerous articles on public policy issues in journals such as *Political Science Quarterly*, *Polity*, *Western Political Quarterly*, *Economic Development Quarterly*, and *Policy Studies Journal*.

CITIZEN GUIDES TO POLITICS AND PUBLIC AFFAIRS
Morgan Marietta and Bert Rockman, Series Editors

Each book in this series is framed around a significant but not well-understood subject that is integral to citizens'—both students and the general public—full understanding of politics and participation in public affairs. In accessible language, these titles provide readers with the tools for understanding the root issues in political life. Individual volumes are brief and engaging, written in short, readable chapters without extensive citations or footnoting. Together they are part of an essential library to equip us all for fuller engagement with the issues of our times.

TITLES IN THE SERIES

**A Citizen's Guide to American Ideology:
Conservatism and Liberalism in Contemporary Politics**
Morgan Marietta

**A Citizen's Guide to the Constitution and the Supreme Court:
Constitutional Conflict in American Politics**
Morgan Marietta

**A Citizen's Guide to American Foreign Policy:
Tragic Choices and the Limits of Rationality**
David Patrick Houghton

**A Citizen's Guide to Deficits and Debt:
The Politics of Taxing, Spending, and Borrowing**
William E. Hudson

A Citizen's Guide to Terrorism and Counterterrorism
Christopher C. Harmon

A CITIZEN'S GUIDE TO DEFICITS AND DEBT

The Politics of Taxing, Spending, and Borrowing

William E. Hudson

Routledge
Taylor & Francis Group

NEW YORK AND LONDON

First published 2014
by Routledge
711 Third Avenue, New York, NY 10017

and by Routledge
2 Park Square, Milton Park, Abingdon, Oxon OX14 4RN

Routledge is an imprint of the Taylor & Francis Group, an informa business

© 2014 Taylor & Francis

Library of Congress Cataloging in Publication Data
Hudson, William E., 1948–
     A citizen's guide to deficits and debt : the politics of taxing, spending, and borrow-
ing / by William E. Hudson.
     pages cm. — (Citizen guides to politics and public affairs)
     Includes bibliographical references and index.
     1. Finance, Public—United States. 2. Government spending policy—United
States. 3. Fiscal policy—United States. 4. United States—Economic
policy—2009– 5. United States—Economic policy—2009– I. Title.
HJ257.3.H83 2013
336.73—dc23
2013025246

ISBN: 978-0-415-64460-0 (hbk)
ISBN: 978-0-415-64461-7 (pbk)
ISBN: 978-0-203-07944-7 (ebk)

Typeset in Garamond
by EvS Communication Networx, Inc.

Printed and bound in the United States of America by Publishers Graphics,
LLC on sustainably sourced paper.

FOR MY CAPSTONE SEMINAR STUDENTS
AND
LORET, ONCE AGAIN

CONTENTS

CONTENTS

ILLUSTRATIONS

Figures

Tables

SERIES EDITORS' FOREWORD

The national debt remains one of our most confusing and intractable political debates. Few citizens can truly claim to understand all of its aspects. *Why is the debt bad for the economy? Why has it accumulated to such heights and why is it so hard to control? Why have our leaders' positions become so entrenched to the point of stalemate? And what is the likely future of the debt struggle?* These questions are answered in clear terms by William Hudson, the Director of Public Administration and Professor of Political Science at Providence College. Author of a popular textbook on American politics (*American Democracy in Peril*, now in its 7th edition), Professor Hudson specializes in the analysis and critique of national policies on economic development, taxation, and social welfare, always from the perspective of citizen engagement in our democracy. He employs his experience in teaching these difficult concepts to dispel the confusion about deficits, debt ceilings, "sequestration," and the misnamed "mandatory" versus "discretionary" spending. Professor Hudson addresses the trade-offs involved in removing various pieces of federal spending that contribute to the national debt, forcing us to examine what is truly at stake and what choices must be made. Contrary to much of the current conversation by our elected leaders, this volume explains why we cannot rely on small reductions in discretionary spending, but must reform the large entitlement programs like Social Security and Medicare as well as re-evaluate our current tax policies if we are to make meaningful changes in the economics of the growing debt.

Perhaps most importantly, Hudson argues that the debates over the national debt are really reflections of a larger conflict over competing visions of America's future. The debt is a master issue that encompasses many smaller conflicts about health care, defense spending, welfare reform, fair levels of taxation, and a host of other public problems that all revolve around the allocation of dollars. Each of these individual questions add up to the largest and most daunting one: What do we really care about as a society? Hudson reveals the competing visions of what Americans should and should not value, reflected in the politics of taxing, spending, and borrowing. The volume explains why we must face these choices about our national priorities, with full knowledge of their true costs and consequences. The era of easy decisions is over. In a time when we can no longer maintain current levels of spending and current levels of taxation along with the old habits of avoiding hard choices, Hudson's *Citizen's Guide* provides us with a clear roadmap to this crucial public debate.

Morgan Marietta and Bert Rockman

ACKNOWLEDGMENTS

The ideas in this book were discussed around the table in two wonderful seminars on *America's Fiscal Future* at Providence College in the spring and fall of 2011. The bright and concerned students in those classes first made me aware of the questions and worries ordinary citizens have about deficits and debt. Without their contributions in those discussions, this book would not have been possible. So I want to thank each by name: Chris Carter, Amanda Flood, Dan Hicks, John Keller, Brittany McHale, Nick Mikula, Dan Roe, Steve Smalley, Danielle Turcotte, Nick Vaz, Kelly Branham, Paul Centofani, Meghan Garry, Zach Gelman, Jillian Kiernan, Danielle Ladd, Dan Malin, Carly Morrison, Mike O'Malley, Justin Smith, Nicole Stuver, and Katy Van de Weghe. Special thanks to my colleague Matt Guardino who made helpful comments that helped me to improve the analysis of the political side to our fiscal situation. I am most grateful to my friend and colleague Bob Trudeau who read and commented on nearly the entire manuscript. His comments greatly improved the clarity of the argument and served to polish my prose. Thanks also to my research assistant, Courtney Buohl, who constructed all the tables and figures, provided copy editing on early drafts, and performed many other research tasks as the book took shape. Morgan Marietta and Bert Rockman made this book possible in their willingness to include this topic in their valuable series of Citizen Guides to Politics and Public Affairs. I appreciate their assistance in advising on this project and for Morgan's comments on my final draft manuscript. My appreciation extends also to Michael Kerns, Darcy Bullock, and the other Routledge staff who made the final product a reality. Thanks as well to Kurt Fenske, Yilin Hou, Greg

Streib, and the anonymous reviewers who examined the initial book proposal. My final thanks go to my dear wife, Loreto Gandara, who, once again, asked gently every day how many pages I had written. Her encouragement and her companionship, when the work was done, made all the effort worthwhile.

INTRODUCTION

Political Conflict over Deficits and Debt: What's It About? What's At Stake?

For the past few years, America has seemed caught up in a monumental struggle over federal deficits and debt. The "fiscal crisis" has become a routine topic of media reports, politicians' speeches, and pundit commentary. Concerns over the minutiae of government budgeting like "entitlements," "tax expenditures," "deficits," and "sequestration" that in the past have been the specialized concern of economists, government accountants, and budget analysts have become fodder for the mass media. These concerns also have been at the center of political conflict as Republican and Democratic politicians face off over how best to put the nation's fiscal house in order.

Pundits and politicians alike cite alarming statistics about the state of the nation's fiscal distress. According to the U.S. Treasury, the federal deficit, at its high point in the years 2009–2011, exceeded $1.3 trillion in each of those years, and thereby contributing to an overall national debt of more than $16 trillion. Levels of federal deficit and debt as a proportion of the overall economy have reached the highest levels since WWII, with debt held by the public exceeding 70 percent of Gross Domestic Product (GDP). Future projections suggest even more alarming developments with the national debt rising to over twice the GDP by mid-century. In light of these widely publicized numbers, according to a 2011 NY Times/CBS poll, American citizens have grown quite alarmed, with 95 percent viewing deficits and debt as a serious problem and 56 percent favoring immediate government action to address it. Yet, citizens have not seen this immediate action to deal with what has been portrayed as a serious national emergency. Instead, for the last several years, rather than solve the debt problem,

1

Republicans and Democrats in Washington seem to be deadlocked in an endless argument over their own different solutions.

For the average citizen this debate seems quite maddening. Why can't those politicians in Washington agree on sensible spending cuts and revenue increases to bring the country's books in balance? Don't ordinary households find reasonable ways to tighten their belts in hard times without breaking up the family? Why not just root out the wasteful spending and cancel unnecessary programs to solve the problem? Why not make the rich pay their fair share of taxes to fund the services we expect from government? Does reducing deficits require changing social insurance programs, like Social Security and Medicare, which Americans earned? Ordinary citizens recoil from the idea of a federal government that runs growing deficits every year. They are alarmed at the prospect of a mounting public debt that will burden future generations. Why is it so hard to find ways to resolve this "fiscal crisis"?

This citizen's guide to federal deficits and debt aims to answer these common sense questions about the politics surrounding America's fiscal future. While at one level dealing with the federal budget seems a matter of simple arithmetic—raising sufficient revenue to match spending commitments or, approached the other way, trimming spending commitments to match available revenue—when examined in a broader context budget politics encompasses nearly the totality of our national political disputes.

Budgets embody value commitments—they express in dollars what the political system deems important. Budgets also reflect the relative power of societal interests. So decisions about how much to tax and spend raise profound questions about who we are and what goals and purposes we wish to pursue as a political community. As reflections of competing political interests, budgetary politics inevitably reflects the clash of interests at the heart of our political system. With fundamental political values and interests at stake, resolving the conflict over deficits and debt cannot be as simple or straightforward as it seems at first glance. In the pages that follow, I will offer a conceptual road map to how the arguments over taxing and spending reflect these larger conflicts of values and interests.

Beyond this clash of values and interests, which is inherent in budgetary conflict at any time, during the past three decades an ideological struggle over competing visions of America's future has spilled over into the debate over deficits and debt. The current arguments over America's debt are the latest round in an old American struggle about the role of government in society. One view sees an active role for the national government in promoting economic development and the well-being of American citizens; the other view is suspicious that a too active government will be a threat to individual liberty.

The contemporary version of this struggle descends from the New Deal era's expansion of the government's role—an expansion furthered in subsequent decades. The new responsibilities that the federal government assumed in the 1930s for regulating the economy, providing basic social benefits, and with the onset of World War II, assuming global national security responsibilities, provided the frame upon which future expansions of government were built. To the present day, public policy controversy has revolved around the extent and scope of these new federal government responsibilities brought on by the New Deal. The recent conflicts come down to arguments about what role we want the federal government to play in the lives of Americans.

Two different portraits of what America is and what its future ought to be underlie this ideological struggle. One portrait envisions an America of rugged individualists who need little from government (or even each other), where government is small, taxation light, and markets unregulated. According to this vision, individual citizens take personal responsibility for their lives—both its opportunities and its risks. This portrait of America has had the rhetorical upper hand in our politics since the election of President Ronald Reagan in 1980, proclaimed wholeheartedly by Republicans and, at times, by Democrats as well. This side usually is labeled "conservative," but its animating ideology, especially when it comes to fiscal matters, is libertarian. From this perspective, if American deficits are high and too much debt threatens, we must reduce government programs and past commitments to citizens. The prudent fiscal course requires cutting government spending.

Several labels might describe the competing ideological portrait— "progressive," "social democratic," or "communitarian" although "liberal" has been the common term used in our political discourse. Franklin Delano Roosevelt's original New Deal, created in the 1930s, had considerable touching up by Lyndon Johnson's Great Society in the 1960s. This vision sees government as a force to provide individuals with economic security and to create a more equitable division of America's prosperity. Many of the budgetary choices and values embedded in the current federal budget stem from this New Deal vision. For the future, this portrait wishes to preserve the New Deal legacy of a strong federal government that promotes individual economic opportunity and also provides ways for citizens to share the life risks any one of us faces. From this perspective, resolving current and future fiscal problems must not threaten this New Deal legacy—even if maintaining it imposes additional tax burdens on citizens.

American politicians are fighting about deficit and debt because Americans are deeply divided over which vision should guide the hands of those who paint the portrait of our future. As we shall see, the choices we make about controlling future spending or raising future taxes will determine which portrait is painted. This book will be a guide to understanding why our on-going fiscal crisis is so important to America's future. The emphasis will be on the source of the crisis in the profound partisan division of the current era and competing visions of the kind of country America should be. By the time the readers reach the last page, I want them to understand that the conflict over deficits and debt is about more than which taxes to increase or what spending to cut. The conflict involves competing visions of the kind of society America will be in the twenty-first century and profound disagreement among Americans about those visions. How we go about resolving the current fiscal crisis will paint a particular portrait of American society in the coming decades.

Before the political roots of the fiscal conflict can be understood, the citizen reader needs a map of how to navigate the federal budget. Part I provides such a map and gives directions on why deficits and debt have become so high in recent years. Most Americans understand little about the composition of federal spending or how the federal government raises revenue. Public ignorance on these matters has to be one of the reasons most citizens find the argument about the budget so baffling. They do not know what exactly politicians are arguing over (and neither, it seems, do some of the politicians). The initial chapters describe the general shape of the spending and revenue sides of the federal budget, introduce the basic vocabulary used in budget policy—including the meaning of "deficit" versus "debt"—and trace the source of the current deficit and debt problems. A critical part of this map also shows how federal budgets are connected to the overall operation of the economy.

This second part, now that the budget map rests firmly implanted in the reader's mind, shifts to explaining the political roots of the fiscal crisis. It takes up the image of competing portraits of America's future as the driver of political conflict over deficits and debt. The four chapters in part II spell out how these competing visions interact within the various parts of the conflict over debt and deficits. Chapter 7 looks at the confrontation between deficit "hawks" and "doves" over whether America's fiscal situation constitutes a "crisis" that demands fundamental alteration in traditional social insurance commitments to citizens. Chapter 8 traces the history of the Republican Party's resistance to raising new tax revenue as a way to lower future debt. Chapter 9 profiles the political conflict over deficit and debt during the Obama years and how it provided an arena for each party to promote its vision of America. Chapter 10 concludes with an analysis of how political conflict over deficits and debt will define which portrait America will become.

Part I

THE SHAPE
OF THE FEDERAL BUDGET

1

FEDERAL DEFICITS AND DEBT

The first step in our citizen's guide to the politics of federal deficits and debt needs to be a definition and description of the key terms themselves. In drawing our map of the federal budget we will begin with several basic questions: Exactly what are the federal deficits? How are they related to the national debt? Do deficits and debt matter? Why? Are deficits and debt wholly bad or do they have a positive side? Government debt, we will see, differs in crucial ways from the debts of individuals and families. When evaluating appropriate levels of government debt, an outlook that regards all debt as somehow immoral clouds our vision of the vital role deficits and debt play in our national economy and society. In this chapter, we will consider the dangers too much debt can bring to our national household, but also look at the benefits that derive from some indebtedness.

What Are Deficits and Debt?

Federal deficits occur when federal government spending in a given year exceeds the amount of tax revenue raised in that year. In other words, deficits represent the shortfall between the money government raises and the amount it spends. To cover this shortfall, the U.S. Treasury must borrow money for the excess expenditure. Hence the connection between deficits and debt: deficits require borrowing which adds to the national debt. The national debt, then, can be thought of as an accumulation of previous deficits.

From whom does the Treasury borrow the money to cover deficits? The answer to this question requires distinguishing between the two parts of the total national debt: the debt held by the public and the debt held by other parts of the national government (intra-governmental holdings). The first and larger portion, the publically held debt, involves the sale of what are called *securities* such as Treasury bonds or savings bonds to investors. Purchasers of these securities do so with the expectation that, after a period of time—at the bonds' maturity date—they can redeem their bonds with interest. The intra-governmental holdings are investments taken out by various governmental funds, the largest of which are the Social Security Trust Fund and Federal Reserve Board. The Social Security Trust Fund holds securities that will be redeemed over the next few decades to cover the retirement costs of the baby boom generation. This is a means of investing the money held in the Social Security Trust Fund so that it grows over time; it simultaneously serves to fund the deficit. The Federal Reserve funds are a tool used to manage the nation's supply of money and credit, the responsibility of the Federal Reserve Board. So, to cover deficits, the U.S. Treasury relies on a combination of borrowing from private investors and from other governmental entities. Because the intra-governmental debt involves obligations from one part of the federal government to another part—all ultimately dependent on the overall taxing and borrowing capacity of the entire federal government—the term national debt usually refers to the publically held portion. It is the debt owed to the public that imposes future interest costs, burdens, and risks that concern those worried about the national debt.

When the Treasury borrows money, it issues Treasury bonds. For example, it will announce the sale of $1,000 bonds at 3 percent interest redeemable in ten years. An investor who purchases a bond, in effect, is loaning the federal government $1,000 (the principal) and receives the 3 percent interest for ten years in addition to being repaid the principal. The amount of interest the U.S. Treasury must pay varies, like any loan, with market conditions—the amount of risk investors associate with Treasury securities and the availability of alternative investments of similar risk. Historically, most investors have seen U.S. Treasuries as an extremely low risk investment (the United States has never defaulted on a loan) and, in recent years, the Treasury has been able to borrow ample amounts of money at relatively low interest rates. Up until now, the federal government never has had any trouble selling Treasury securities to cover budget deficits.

Who are the investors that purchase these bonds—who "owns" the national debt? They can be anyone who wishes to make the investment. Until recently, the American people owned nearly all the national debt. Owners include corporations, pension funds, insurance companies, state and local governments, and individual citizens.[1] Anyone with a balanced investment portfolio probably owns some Treasury bonds. Anyone who has ever received a U.S. savings bond from a grandparent owns a piece of the national debt.

Foreign investors, both foreign governments and individuals, can also purchase Treasury bonds and, in recent years, have been eager to do so: they now own nearly 50 percent of the publically held debt. This is a recent development; until the mid-1990s foreigners held only about 20 percent of the national debt. Around that time many foreign governments and foreign nationals found investment in U.S. Treasury bonds a safe investment in a volatile world economy—particularly the Chinese government, which has held about $1 trillion in U.S. debt for the past several years. The turmoil in the financial markets after 2008 increased the demand for U.S. securities as investors sought a safe investment. The extent of foreign ownership of the debt has two contrasting sides. On the one hand, it shows that U.S. Treasuries are one of the soundest investments in the world economy; on the other, it makes our national treasury dependent on the continued confidence of foreign governments. With so much of our debt financed by foreign governments, some people worry that these foreign loans might be used as a threat to influence American foreign policy or, if foreign governments suddenly were to demand repayment, precipitate a fiscal crisis.

Debt, Deficits, and the Economy

The American public usually blames politicians for existing levels of deficit and debt. Some social critics also point the finger of blame at the American people themselves for demanding generous spending programs while also insisting that taxes be kept low. Whether the blame is aimed at politicians or the public, both of these accusations assume that levels of deficit and debt are mostly the consequence of conscious spending and taxing policy decisions. And to a large extent, this is true. The taxing and spending choices made over the past several decades have established a fiscal framework that encourages growing debt. However, this is not the whole story. Levels of deficit and debt are also a function of economic performance. When the national economy is strong, deficits tend to shrink and the national debt normally declines. When the economy does poorly, the reverse happens with a vengeance.

The interaction of policy choices and economic growth can be seen through a walk through the history of deficits and debt in the post-World War II period.[2] Figures 1.1 and 1.2 compare debt and deficits since the 1940s to the total size—output of goods and services—of the economy, the Gross Domestic Product (GDP). As we can see from Figure 1.1, the high point of national debt was World War II, when the federal government ran successive huge deficits to fund the war effort, raising the debt over 100 percent of the GDP. Notice how steadily, however, that massive debt was brought down over the next two decades. How did that happen—especially since the federal government continued to run deficits most years (see Figure 1.2)? The answer was an economy that grew faster than the rate of debt growth. A growing economy during the post-WWII period allowed the reduction in

Source: Compiled by author with data from U.S. Office of Management and Budget. *Fiscal Year 2014 Budget of the U.S. Government: Historical Tables.* April 10, 2013. http://www.whitehouse.gov/sites/default/files/omb/budget/fy2014/assets/hist.pdf

Figure 1.1 National Debt as a Percentage of GDP, 1940–2012

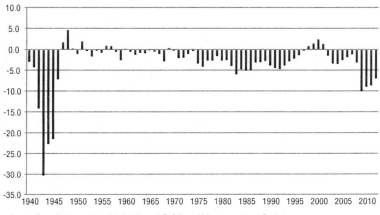

Source: Compiled by author with data from U.S. Office of Management and Budget.
Fiscal Year 2014 Budget of the U.S. Government: Historical Tables.
April 10, 2013. http://www.whitehouse.gov/sites/default/files/omb/budget/fy2014/assets/hist.pdf

Figure 1.2   Deficits or Surpluses as a Percentage of GDP, 1940–2012

debt relative to GDP even as deficits added to the total debt amount. Of course, fiscal restraint also was a factor as the gap between spending and revenue was relatively small during deficit years and there were a few years of budget surplus. The two decades after World War II demonstrate that while appropriate taxing and spending policies matter for restraining deficits and debt, the most important policies during the period were those that promoted strong economic growth.

This era of declining national debt came to an end in the mid-1970s as several years of economic stagnation, including three severe recessions, increased deficits and debt. These economic doldrums automatically increased deficits as tax revenue fell during the recessions and spending on unemployment compensation and other income support programs went up along with stimulus spending to restore economic growth. Even though modest economic growth returned in the 1980s, the Reagan administration policies of a large cut in tax rates but also increased spending, particularly on a massive arms buildup, led to large deficits and a substantial increase in the national debt. National debt in relation to the economy doubled from a post-WWII low of 24 percent of GDP in 1975 to about 50 percent in the early 1990s. By the mid-1990s during the Clinton administration, a combination of higher taxes, spending restraint, and a post-1995 economic boom brought deficits and the debt down, producing four years of budget surpluses after 1998 for the first time since 1969. A mild recession in 2000 undercut this positive development, but the fiscal pressure only increased when the George W. Bush administration enacted massive tax cuts and initiated wars in Afghanistan and Iraq. Weak economic growth throughout the Bush years compounded the deficit bias of the tax and spending policies. Even before the financial crisis of 2008, the national debt was expanding at a record rate.

The economic collapse of 2008—the Great Recession—has had a devastating impact on deficits and debt. As typically occurs in a recession, tax revenue declined by about $500 billion to the smallest level of GDP, 15 percent, since 1950. At the same time, expenditures rose for unemployment compensation and increases in various safety net programs like Medicaid and Food Stamps as more people, because of their declining incomes, qualified for the programs. In addition, both the Bush administration, in 2008, and the Obama administration, in 2009, enacted economic stimulus measures to restore economic growth. First, the controversial $700 billion Troubled Asset Relief Program (TARP) enacted in the waning days of the Bush administration injected capital into the banks to forestall a financial collapse. Although financial institutions would repay much of the TARP funds, the program temporarily added to deficits from 2009 to 2011. Second, both the Bush and Obama administrations enacted packages of tax cuts and spending increases to stimulate the economy. The largest of these was the $788 billion American Recovery and Reinvestment Act, the "Obama stimulus." The result of the combination of economic downturn and stimulus spending was four years of greater than $1 trillion deficits and an increase in the national debt to close to 70 percent of GDP.

To many Americans, the alarming rise in debt and deficit during the recession called into question the Obama stimulus. For families across America who were responding to their own economic crises by cutting back spending, the idea that the federal government was expanding spending in response to the crisis seemed wrong. Many asked: "If we have to tighten our belts in a recession, shouldn't the government tighten its belt too?" The question draws an analogy between a family budget and the federal budget and assumes that both ought to respond to economic hard times in the same way. Defenders of the stimulus argued that the belt tightening analogy was misguided. As economic theorist John Maynard Keynes argued in his 1936 classic *General Theory of Employment, Interest, and Money*, national economies are different from family economies—restoring prosperity to depressed national economies demanded loosening not tightening the national belt.

Prior to Keynes, most economists and policy makers embraced the belt-tightening analogy as the appropriate way to respond to an economic downturn. They assumed that government could do little to restore economic growth and a balanced budget was the best government response to hard times. In accordance with this outlook, the Hoover administration, as did other governments around the world, reacted to the onset of the Great Depression in 1930 with fiscal austerity—tax increases and spending cuts to balance the budget. The expectation was that eventually the economy would begin growing on its own as falling wages would make hiring workers affordable to business. Despite this expectation, government belt tightening caused high unemployment and falling wages to worsen. The common sense response of belt tightening fiscal austerity in economic hard times did not work.

Keynes' novel theory of the national economy explained why fiscal austerity was not working and guided fiscal policy response to recessions in subsequent decades. The reason unemployment persisted, according to Keynes, was that, with so many consumers unemployed and earning low wages, there were fewer and fewer consumers able to buy what businesses produced. With low consumer demand, businesses had no incentive to invest in the production of new products and therefore did not hire new workers. The result was a circular process, a vicious cycle, where high unemployment sapped consumer demand, leading businesses not to produce goods, leading to more unemployment, undermining future demand in a never-ending downward spiral. To break this spiral, Keynes argued that government had to step in and create demand by injecting money into the economy through higher spending, tax cuts, or a combination of both. In other words, government deficits in an economic downturn were a positive force to restore economic growth.

This Keynesian analysis viewed government deficits in a new light. Instead of a moral failure to keep spending in line with revenue, deficits could be a positive factor in restoring economic growth. Keynes understood that, from the perspective of the economy as a whole, one family's spending was another family's income. As all families tightened their belts in a recession and reduced spending, they simultaneously reduced the income of other families as businesses laid off workers because of insufficient sales of their products. For the good of the economy as a whole, when everyone else was tightening their belts, government needed to loosen its belt.

From this point of view, the rise in deficits after 2008 should not be viewed with alarm but seen as the best response to the recession. Even though the stimulus temporarily added to the deficit and debt, not to do so would have prolonged and deepened the economic downturn, making deficits and debt even worse in the long run. (Europeans, after 2008, largely rejected Keynesian solutions, pursuing austerity policies aimed at immediate reduction of government deficits. The result has been continued economic stagnation, much worse than in the United States and higher deficits. Great Britain's austerity policies, for example, drove its economy into a second recession and increased its debt.)

Of course, everyone did not view the large deficits of Obama's first term in this Keynesian light. On the political Right, Republican critics vehemently condemned the Obama stimulus package, blaming it for making the economy worse. Their position showed the continuing attraction, despite the experience of the 1930s, of the belt tightening metaphor, and fiscal austerity as the appropriate response to recessions. Anger over the stimulus and rising deficits were major factors leading to the rise of the Tea Party movement (along with opposition to Obama's health care plan). This anger, combined with a continuing sluggish economy, led to Republican victories in 2010 and a Republican majority in the House of Representatives. The Obama stimulus also had critics on the left who claimed continued economic sluggishness was a result of a stimulus that was too small. These critics argued that the severity of the recession demanded a much larger Keynesian stimulus than what was enacted.

Good and Bad Deficits

If one accepts Keynesian theory, deficits sometimes are good: in fact, they are the essential remedy when the economy crashes. Running a deficit temporarily in a recession and adding to debt should restore economic growth, which will improve the future national fiscal balance. Without such stimulus spending, the negative impact of a recession on government revenues and spending would make the government's fiscal condition even worse. Deficit spending in a recession and the resulting rise in the debt is a kind of emergency spending that forestalls greater harm and can be made up in the future. Besides economic stimulus, one should put spending on other national emergencies like wars or natural disasters in this category. As Figure 1.1 shows, the United States ran up its debt enormously during WWII, but few would regard that increase as either a waste or harmful. The war debt preserved our national security and freedom, making possible post-war economic prosperity that easily paid down that debt. Increasing government debt in an emergency is akin to someone putting an emergency car repair on a credit card in order to have transportation to get to work. That debt permits that person to continue to work, preventing loss of income, and eventually allowing him or her to pay off the debt.

Besides adding to debt in emergencies, public investments are another type of expenditure that can reasonably be put on the public credit card. These investments in economic infrastructure, such as roads, airports, education, or a modernized electrical grid, pay for themselves over time in future economic growth. The cost of the interstate highway system, for example, which added to the federal debt in the 1950s and 60s, has paid for itself many times over in added economic productivity. Using debt to pay for investments in physical (roads) and human (education) capital also can be justified because the benefits of the expenditure are spread over many years. A state government that issues debt to add a new campus to the state university system creates a facility that will serve students far into the future as the debt is being repaid. It would be absurd to make the first students enrolled pay the entire cost of the campus out of huge tuition payments or a single year tax increase rather than spread the cost into the future through debt repayments. Just like families who take out a mortgage to pay for a house they will live in for many years as they pay down the mortgage, public investments involve taking on debt now to provide benefits for future citizens. To the extent our national debt was incurred for such public investments, we are simply paying our share for the benefits we enjoy from those investments. Viewed in this way, the national debt includes pieces of the highways we drive on, the costs of dams and power plants that produce our electricity, the education of our parents and grandparents that contribute to our own standard of living, and costs of wars that have preserved our freedom.

So, while we should not regard all deficits and debt as bad, we still might have reason to be concerned when debt seems to grow not in response to emergencies or when it seems to grow larger than can be justified as a support to public investments. In recent years, many observers have been concerned with the increase in the *structural deficit*. These are deficits that occur even in times of economic growth simply because insufficient tax revenue is being generated to pay for existing spending commitments. The concern for structural deficits arose in the wake of the large Reagan tax reductions in 1981 and the similar Bush tax cuts in 2001 and 2003. Although justified as "supply-side" tax cuts that would generate additional growth that would prevent any adverse impact on the deficit, they failed to produce such a spurt in growth and, because there were no offsetting spending reductions, there were large budget deficits (see Figure 2.1). In addition, the aging of the population, rising health costs, and the needs of the economic disadvantaged have produced increased spending on entitlement programs like Social Security, Medicare, and Medicaid. Unlike public investment spending, government spending on entitlements is a form of consumption that does not contribute necessarily to future economic growth. However worthwhile these public consumption expenditures are, if not paid for with existing revenues, they add to the national debt. The growing structural deficits resulting from these tax cuts and entitlement costs, even before the Great Recession of 2008, have contributed to growing debt. As we will see in subsequent chapters, projections show the national debt exploding in future decades.

What is the downside of the national debt? Why should we worry if debt keeps rising? Budget experts generally identify three main consequences of rising debt.[3] First, rising debt, even modest rises, tends to be a drag on economic growth because public borrowing crowds out private investment. If domestic investors put their capital into Treasury bonds, that capital is not available for private investment. Lower investment in new business activity means slower economic growth and lower incomes over the long run. But what if the debt were financed with foreign rather than domestic capital, as increasingly has been the case? Wouldn't that diminish the crowding out of domestic investment? Foreign investment can counter the crowding out effect of rising debt both by soaking up some of that debt and by boosting private investment, but these offsetting effects come at a cost. The profits and income from these foreign investments will flow abroad rather than contributing to increasing the standard of living of Americans. Whether rising national debt crowds out domestic private investment or is underwritten from abroad the effect is the same—diminished future American prosperity.

Second, rising debt also has a direct impact on the federal budget. As debt grows, so does the proportion of federal spending that must be devoted to paying the interest on that debt. Growing interest payments leave less revenue available for other public expenditures such as spending on infrastructure investments like education or highway systems and meeting the needs of the elderly and disadvantaged. The effect is the same as an individual running up large credit card debt: more and more of one's income goes to credit card interest rather than to the necessities of life. Of course, a new, higher paying job would go a long way toward easing the pain of credit card interest payments, but such a convenient boost to income usually is not easily available to most individuals. But government is different: it has direct control over its level of income through the power to tax. However, covering higher interest payments with higher taxes is not cost free. Citizens might resist paying these higher taxes and, even if government officials managed to impose higher taxes anyway, these taxes would drain resources from the private economy contributing again to slower economic growth. But does not reducing future debt itself require raising taxes or cutting spending? Wouldn't the impact be the same? Most analysts argue that during periods of prosperity tax increases and spending cuts to forestall raising debt would be much smaller and less onerous than what would be needed to cope with rising interest costs from a ballooning future debt. The strategy would be to impose small discomforts with fiscal discipline today to prevent much larger pain in the future. Of course, as Keynes reminds us, such austerity only makes sense when the economy is growing, not during a recession.

Third, if national debt grows too large, the nation has less capacity to respond to emergencies such as economic recessions, to a financial crisis such as the one in 2008, or even to wars. Sometimes deficit spending is required, as argued earlier, to respond to emergencies. If in times of such emergency the nation already faced a huge debt burden, the costs of adding to that burden would be greater. Political resistance to even needed emergency expenditures would be high if politicians and citizens feared the costs of added debt in terms of cutbacks in existing programs or higher future taxes. Some argue that such fears already have had an effect in the form of too much government austerity in the wake of the Great Recession. Even as the economy faltered with weak growth in 2011 and 2012, the Obama administration found little support for additional stimulus spending. Republicans in Congress raised the specter of rising national debt as a rationale for resisting any further stimulus, an argument that seemed to resonate with much of the public. In summer of 2011, the Republican House majority leader even went so far as to denounce increasing the deficit to pay the costs of covering of the emergency response to Hurricane Irene. If this resistance to emergency spending emerged when the national debt was at about 60 percent of GDP, how much greater would they be if the debt rose to 100 or more percent of GDP? Lower debt provides more flexibility when national emergency requires increasing it.

Conclusion

Debt then has both virtues and dangers. Incurring debt to finance public investments to support economic growth and future well-being is both sensible and wise. Like a family taking out a mortgage or a student taking out a college loan, the federal government should borrow to fund the physical and human capital essential to future prosperity. Also, making future generations pay part of the cost of investments from which they will benefit makes both economic and moral sense. Increasing debt in response to emergencies, like economic recessions, also makes sense as a means to prevent even greater economic and future fiscal pain. At the same time, debt has its dangers. A growing national debt, even if it might result in part from wise public investments and prudent emergency spending, can, at a certain, level itself undermine economic growth and prosperity. Debt brought on by structural deficits due to low taxes and high public consumption today creates a risk that coping with the resulting debt will require the reverse in the future.

Deficits and debt then have a Goldilocks aspect. Debt, like the bowl of porridge that is "just right," needs to be sufficient to meet our public needs but not so high as to threaten our future economic prosperity. The political conflict over deficit and debt partly involves an argument about what is "just right." Americans have different tolerances regarding levels of debt risk. Moreover, Americans differ over how to get to just the right amount of debt. Some, usually Democrats, would get there through raising sufficient revenue to meet spending commitments; others, usually Republicans, would pare down those spending commitments rather than raise tax revenues.

These different approaches to getting to "just right" stem from the contemporary ideological divide. Democrats see a large, robust, and active government as essential to the general welfare of all Americans. Republicans view such a government as a threat to individual freedom and wish to constrain it. The heated conflict over deficits and debt in recent years, then, is about much more than finding the porridge bowl that tastes just right. As we shall see, particularly in part II, it is a battle about the size and shape of the bowl itself. Before we take up that battle of the bowls, however, we need to get a clearer idea of content of federal spending and taxing and how it has evolved over the past several decades. That is the purpose of the next few chapters.

Notes

1. The U.S. Department of the Treasury issues regular bulletins on the status of the national debt, including ownership information. The bulletin can be accessed online at http://www.fms.treas.gov/bulletin/index.html. The Bureau of Public Debt also maintains a FAQ site about all aspects of the national debt including links to other information sites: http://www.treasurydirect.gov/govt/resources/faq/faq_publicdebt.htm.

2. Budget data cited are from Office of Management and Budget. *Budget of the U.S. Government Fiscal Year 2013: Historical Tables.* February 13, 2012 (http://www.whitehouse.gov/sites/default/files/omb/budget/fy2013/assets/hist.pdf).

3. Congressional Budget Office. "Federal Debt and the risk of a Fiscal Crisis." *CBO Economic and Budget Issue Brief.* July 27, 2010 (http://cbo.gov/sites/default/files/cbofiles/ftpdocs/116xx/doc11659/07-27_debt_fiscalcrisis_brief.pdf).

2

BUDGET PIES

An Overview of Federal Spending and Revenue

Most Americans are worried about the federal government's rising deficits and debt. Recent Gallup polls show that over 80 percent of Americans say they worry either a great deal or a fair amount about the country's fiscal condition. Most feel federal deficits ought to be reduced immediately and tend to favor cutting spending as the method of doing so. Yet fewer citizens seem to understand much about how government spends taxpayer money and how the pattern of that spending itself poses a challenge to addressing deficits and debt. Understanding how the federal government spends taxpayer dollars and how it goes about raising those dollars is the first step needed to guide citizens through the intricacies of deficit and debt politics. This chapter provides a quick tour of the overall shape of federal spending and taxing, setting the stage for more detailed examinations in the chapters that follow.

To establish a clear picture in our minds of what the government spends and where it gets its money, we will use the familiar device of pie graphs to show the broad categories of federal government spending and the source of federal revenues in a recent budget year—fiscal 2011. The pie in Figure 2.1 shows how spending is divided, and Figure 2.2 shows the revenue contributions of different taxes. Through a careful review of these pies and their slices, we can begin to understand what is at stake in political debates over reducing deficits and debt. In particular, we can begin to see the value choices involved in the deficit and debt debate. If we are going to reduce deficits by cutting spending, what will have to be cut and what impacts will that have on citizens? If raising taxes is the solution, what taxes can be raised and who will pay them? The Figures 2.1 and 2.2 give us a start to answering these questions.

Federal Spending

The starting points for understanding the spending pie (Figure 2.1) are the portions marked *mandatory* spending and *discretionary* spending. The discretionary portion of the pie marks the part of the budget Congress can alter in its annual appropriations to government agencies in the annual budget process. This spending is open to congressional modification in any given fiscal year. The spending pie's larger mandatory portion funds programs Congress has authorized to provide specific benefits but whose annual cost cannot be controlled through the annual appropriations process. Because they fund specific benefits to individuals already authorized by law, spending for them occurs automatically without specific congressional budget authorization. These programs sometimes are referred to as *entitlement* programs since the legislation authorizing these benefits conveys a legal entitlement to them. For these entitlements, the amount of spending on them in a given year depends on the specific benefits promised and the number of people legally entitled to these benefits.

The two largest of these programs, Social Security and Medicare, illustrate how spending to support them can be considered mandatory.

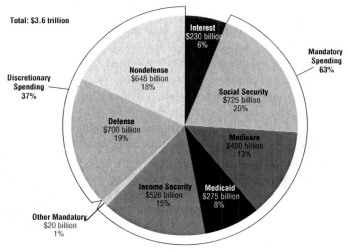

Source: Compiled by author with data from U.S. Office of Management and Budget. *Fiscal Year 2013 Budget of the U.S. Government: Historical Tables.* February 13, 2012. http://www.whitehouse.gov/sites/default/files/omb/budget/fy2013/assets/hist.pdf

Figure 2.1   Federal Spending, Fiscal Year 2011

The authorizing legislation that created Social Security, which consists of the Social Security Act of 1935 plus its many amendments over the years, defines the categories of individuals entitled to receive benefits: in this case, qualified retirees, disabled workers, and deceased qualified workers' spouses and children. It also defines the amount of benefits to be paid to them. So, the amount of Social Security spending in a given year depends on the level of Social Security benefit payments promised to beneficiaries in the Social Security Act and the number of retired people, survivors, and disabled people eligible to receive those benefits. Likewise in Medicare, the level of spending depends on the number of elderly people insured by the program who receive medical services in a given year and the cost of those services. In neither of these cases can Congress control how much must be spent on these programs through the normal budget process; hence, these can be considered mandatory expenditures. To alter mandatory spending requires amending the underlying legislation authorizing the spending. Congress could, of course, at any time repeal or alter this authorizing legislation, reducing promised benefits or those eligible for benefits. So, spending labeled mandatory is mandatory only in the sense that it cannot be changed through the annual appropriations process. Discretionary spending, in contrast, always can be altered through either cutting or increasing agency budgets.

Notice that of the two categories of spending, the mandatory spending slices comprised nearly two-thirds of the budget pie in 2011, while discretionary spending, the defense and non-defense slice equaled 38 percent. This fact alone constitutes a basic fact confronting those who would reduce federal deficits through spending cuts. If cuts in spending are to be made quickly in the budget process without addressing entitlements, they must come from the smaller discretionary portion of the pie. For those who would prefer these cuts not come from national defense, they must obtain reductions from the small non-defense discretionary 18 percent slice amounting to $646 billion in 2011. Even if deficit cutters had been moved, in that year, to the extreme of cutting all spending in this category (and thereby wiping out most of the federal government), they would have reduced the $1.3 trillion deficit only by half. The budget pie shows unmistakably that any serious approach to reducing deficits through spending cuts has to address mandatory entitlement programs.

The challenge of dealing with the deficit through mandatory spending cuts becomes clearer if we examine this portion of the budget pie in more detail. Two of the biggest slices on the mandatory portion of the pie, making up 35 percent of the total budget pie, go to supporting primarily the needs of the elderly through Social Security and Medicare. Any attempt to cut the deficit through cuts in these programs would require not only reducing benefits that most Americans need and well deserve but also would require defying a powerful voting constituency.

Much of the balance of the mandatory portion is for programs that constitute what is often referred to as the safety net for the poor. Unlike Social Security and Medicare, which provide entitled benefits irrespective of wealth or income, these safety net programs are *means-tested*, that is, entitlement depends on one's total assets and income being below a certain amount. The largest of these means-tested entitlements is Medicaid—about 8 percent of the pie. The "other" category on the pie contains several important means-tested safety net programs such as Supplemental Nutritional Assistance Program (SNAP), popularly known as food stamps, the Earned Income Tax Credit (EITC), housing, and energy assistance. Unlike Medicare and Social Security, cutting these programs to reduce the deficit would not involve facing up to a powerful political constituency, but they would undermine the well-being of the poorest, most vulnerable group of Americans.

Means-tested entitlements account for about half of the spending in the "other" category. The second half includes spending for unemployment compensation, which cost about $117 billion in 2011 and federal employee retirement. In addition, about 6 percent of the budget in 2011 was spent on interest and, while set apart from the mandatory portion on the pie, this spending also is mandatory because it must be paid to the federal government's creditors. Although a relatively small slice in 2011, we will see in chapter 6 that the interest slice is slated to grow quickly as the overall national debt grows in the future.

On the discretionary portion of the pie, national defense stands out as a major budgetary commitment. The second-largest slice in the overall pie comprises the $700 billion spent in 2011 on national security. This includes funds for paying and supporting members of the armed forces, contracts to the defense industry to purchase weapons systems, and maintaining military bases, and naval deployments around the world. The last remaining slice—non-defense discretionary spending,

18 percent of the total—pays for everything else the federal government does. This includes much of what most of us think of when we think of the federal government and federal spending. This portion pays the salaries of the federal civilian workforce including FBI agents, air traffic controllers, national park rangers, and environmental scientists. It also includes the budgets of the all the federal agencies providing critical services to the country, such as, the Centers for Disease Control (CDC), the Census Bureau, the Weather Service, and the Federal Emergency Management Agency (FEMA). This small slice also funds all the grants to state and local governments for supporting education, building and repairing roads and bridges, or operating airports. The infamous "earmarks," never more than about 1 percent of the total budget, also come from this non-defense discretionary slice. These also are the funds that support the operation of the three branches of government: Congress, including all congressional and staff salaries; the presidency; and the Supreme Court. When most Americans think of the federal government, they are likely to think of activities such as these even though they constitute less than one-fifth of all federal spending.

A final type of spending which has significant impact on federal deficits does not appear on the budget pies—*tax expenditures*.[1] From the inception of the income tax in 1913, the tax law has allowed taxpayers to exclude certain income from taxation, deduct some personal spending from the calculation of taxable income, or receive a credit applied to the taxpayer's final tax bill for certain kinds of personal expenditures. These tax expenditures now include the employee contribution to employer-provided health insurance (the largest exclusion in the tax code), the deduction for home mortgage interest payments, and the child tax credit. These many exclusions, deductions, and credits remove from the revenue pie about $1 trillion in revenue (in 2011) that otherwise would end up in the U.S. Treasury. (These are explained in more detail in chapter 5.)

Spending and American Values

The budget pie not only shows what the federal government spends, it also provides insight into what American society values. The shape of the budget results from policy choices made over decades in creating programs and establishing commitments. The pie looks the way it does because elected officials have made choices about what to value and how public revenues will support those values. When we look at the pie this way, what does it tell us about what the American government values?

First, the federal government places a high value on national security as shown in the one-fifth of the budget devoted to defense. As we shall see, this has been a long standing commitment since World War II and probably cannot be expected to diminish too much in the future. Second, spending over one-third of the budget on Social Security and Medicare shows a strong commitment to caring for the needs of the elderly. Older Americans are the prime beneficiaries of entitlement spending. Third, the budget commits substantial resources to supporting the incomes of individuals. Income support programs for the poor, disabled, retired, and unemployed (add together the other and the Social Security slice) constitute, again, over one-third of the pie. The federal government plays a major role in supplementing the distribution of national income in the economic marketplace with payments to those who are disadvantaged in that distribution. Finally, despite recent controversy over "government-run health care," the federal government already commits substantial resources to providing health care—fully 29 percent of the budget if we combine spending on Medicare and Medicaid. If we added to these spending from discretionary spending on veterans and military health programs, medical research, and federal public health expenditures, the percentage would be larger. So, in sum, based on analysis of the budget pie, what does the federal government mainly do and what does it value? It protects our country from foreign threats, cares for Americans in their old age, supports the incomes of those in need, and provides health care to the sick.

Federal Revenues

The revenue pie (Figure 2.2) shows us the other side of the budgetary picture. The first point to note is that, in 2011, the federal government raised only two-thirds of the revenue needed to fund spending for that year. This revenue shortfall, of course, defines the deficit, which was about $1.3 trillion. Individual income taxes made up the largest pie slice—a fact not surprising to many Americans who think first of

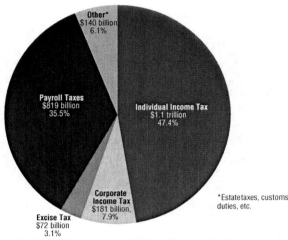

Source: Compiled by author with data from U.S. Office of Management and Budget.
Fiscal Year 2013 Budget of the U.S. Government: Historical Tables. February 13, 2012.
http://www.whitehouse.gov/sites/default/files/omb/budget/fy2013/assets/hist.pdf

Figure 2.2   Federal Revenues, Fiscal Year 2011

the income tax when they think of federal taxes. What might surprise many, however, is the size of the "social insurance taxes" slice, which is close in size to the income tax slice. Federal income taxes provided about 48 percent of tax revenues and social insurance taxes about 36 percent. These latter taxes are the FICA payroll taxes workers have deducted from their paychecks for Social Security and Medicare, which have grown considerably in the last three decades as a source of federal revenue. Many Americans might be surprised at the small corporate income tax slice. Corporations provide only about 8 percent in federal revenues and, contrary to payroll taxes, have contributed a steadily diminishing proportion of tax funds. The other slice, just below 10 percent, covers a variety of other revenues such as excise taxes and customs duties.

What about the $1.3 trillion revenue shortfall? How is that covered? The answer is through issuing new government debt in the form of sales of Treasury securities. As explained in the previous chapter, these securities are sold to a variety of investors including individuals, foreign governments, corporations and mutual funds, and state and local governments. These sales to cover budget deficits are added on to the accumulating national debt.

Growth in Spending and Taxes

Many Americans seem to believe that rising deficits and debt are a consequence of an explosion in government spending in recent years. They also think the overall burden of taxation has increased. The perception of rising government spending results, in part, from the impact of the recession and the efforts of both the Bush and Obama administrations to stimulate the economy. As was explained in the previous chapter, this short-term impact on spending and deficits will abate as the economy recovers. Perceptions of exploding government spending result as well from the raw budget numbers some commentators and the media use to report the growth in spending. The $3.6 trillion of spending in 2011 seems an enormous figure to most of us, as did the pre-recession $2.6 trillion in 2007. Compared with much smaller levels of spending as recently as the late 1980s when federal spending totaled about $1 trillion, one-third as much as today, suggests a massive expansion of government. And when compared to as far back as the early 1960s, when total spending reached only in the $100 billion range, today's spending level appears gargantuan. The same goes with revenue figures. The rise in total government revenues expressed in absolute terms from about $92 billion in 1962 to the $2.3 trillion in 2011 implies a gouging increase in federal taxes.

These absolute numbers, of course, distort the reality of the growth of government spending and taxation. First, they ignore inflation's cumulative impact over time on these numbers. The lower value of the dollar in 1962 or even 1989 makes the budget figures of today seem much larger than they actually are in comparison. Second, and perhaps more significantly, the American economy has expanded tremendously over the past half century. In 1960 the total Gross Domestic Product (GDP), the total output of goods and services in the economy, amounted to only about $500 billion and GDP was a little over $5 trillion in the late 1980s. Today's GDP of around $15 trillion is three times larger than it was just two decades ago. This growth in GDP has significance for evaluating growth in federal spending and taxes. A growing GDP means an automatic increase in tax revenues going to the government as individuals earn higher incomes. Also, a growing economy demands higher levels of government expenditure to support it and the needs of the growing population that accompanies economic growth. To realistically assess the growth of government spending and taxes, we need to account for both the effect of inflation and GDP growth. Only then can we have a clear answer to whether government spending and taxes have become more burdensome.

The best way to do this, as shown in Figure 2.3, is to show the growth of taxes and spending in relation to GDP over time. The story this figure tells is not of a massively expanding government, but rather one of long-term stability in both spending and taxing in comparison to the overall economy. Since the early 1960s, government revenues have fluctuated in a narrow range around about 18 percent of GDP. Government spending has been a bit higher, reflecting the continuing deficit spending over most of the period, and fluctuated a bit more widely ranging from about 18 percent of GDP to the low 20 percents. We can see that the Great Recession has had a major impact on both government spending and revenues producing a record high, since the 1940s, in spending relative to GDP of 25 percent in 2009 dropping off to about 24 percent for the last few years.

The increase in the relative size of government spending results from a combination of increased spending, including the Obama stimulus programs, unemployment compensation, and other safety net expenditures, and a decline in the size of the overall economy. This

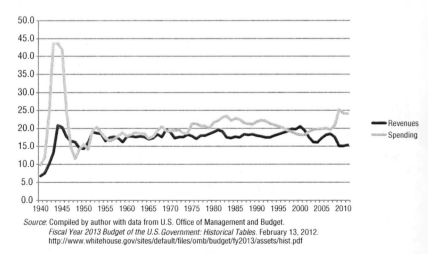

Source: Compiled by author with data from U.S. Office of Management and Budget.
Fiscal Year 2013 Budget of the U.S. Government: Historical Tables. February 13, 2012.
http://www.whitehouse.gov/sites/default/files/omb/budget/fy2013/assets/hist.pdf

Figure 2.3   Revenues and Spending as Percentages of GDP, 1940–2011

24 percent figure is only slightly higher than spending relative to GDP in the last major recession in the early Reagan administration of the 1980s. Tax revenues, by contrast, have fallen dramatically relative to GDP reaching 15 percent of GDP, a level not seen since 1950. The economic downturn dramatically cut into American's incomes, thus reducing federal tax revenue. Projections suggest that as economic growth returns, relative tax and spending levels, at least in the short term, will return to close to pre-recession levels. These data provide no support for the idea of a huge explosion in underlying non-recession related spending and taxes.

Changing Composition of Spending and Taxes

While the overall size of spending and taxes, relative to GDP, has remained fairly stable over the past few decades, there have been dramatic changes in the composition of both. The spending story revolves around the expansion of mandatory spending relative to discretionary spending, in particular non-defense discretionary spending. The tax story is the increase in the importance of payroll taxes for federal revenues and the decline in the corporate income tax. Table 2.1 shows that in 1962 discretionary spending took up about two-thirds of the federal budget and mandatory spending plus interest comprised the other third. Today these percentages have been reversed. In 2011, discretionary spending made up 37 percent of the budget and mandatory plus interest equaled 63 percent. Mandatory spending, excluding interest, has expanded greatly over this time period from about one-fourth of the budget in 1962 compared to 56 percent today. Compared to fifty years ago, the federal government spends a much smaller percentage of its budget for national defense. In 1962, defense discretionary spending ate up nearly half of the entire budget compared to only 20 percent today. Non-defense discretionary spending has held fairly steady over this period, taking up about the same percentage of the budget as it did in 1962. The shifts among broad budget categories over time has everything to do with increased emphasis on spending for social insurance programs like Social Security and Medicare and less relative emphasis on military expenditures (although absolute spending on the military, even controlling for inflation, has been quite high recently—as we shall see in chapter 4).

Table 2.1 Percentage of Spending Distribution Over Time

Fiscal Year	Discretionary		Mandatory	Net Interest
	National Defense	Non-Defense	Total	
1962	49.2	18.3	26.1	6.4
1970	41.9	19.6	31.2	7.4
1980	22.8	24.0	44.4	8.9
1990	24.0	16.0	45.3	14.7
2000	16.5	17.9	53.2	12.5
2003	18.7	19.4	54.7	7.1
2005	20.0	19.2	53.4	7.4
2007	20.1	18.1	53.1	8.7
2009	18.7	16.5	59.5	5.3
2011	19.4	18.0	56.2	6.4

Source: Compiled by author with data from U.S. Office of Management and Budget. Fiscal Year 2013 Budget of the U.S. Government: Historical Tables. February 13, 2012. http://www.white house.gov/sites/default/files/omb/budget/fy2013/assets/hist.pdf.

Table 2.2 shows shifts in sources of tax revenue over this same period. Most dramatic has been the relative decline of corporate taxes as a source of government revenue. In the early 1960s, corporations provided nearly one-fifth of government revenues; today, corporate taxes make up only 8 percent—less than half of fifty years ago. The drop in the corporate percentage of overall revenues began in the 1970s and continued for the next four decades. In effect, payroll taxes have replaced corporate taxes over the past forty years. Social insurance payroll taxes provided only about 17 percent of all revenues fifty years ago, but now provide over one-third. Income taxes have held fairly steady over this period providing just under one-half of all revenue.

As we will explore in more detail in chapter 5, this shift toward payroll taxes represents an overall shift in the tax burden toward the middle class and from taxation of capital income to taxation of labor income. Income tax rates are progressive—taxing a higher proportion of one's income as income rises. The income tax also taxes all income both wages and investment income, the latter primarily earned by higher income earners. In contrast, payroll taxes are regressive because of the ceiling on the amount of income they tax and are imposed only on wage

Table 2.2 Percentage of Revenue Over Time

Fiscal Year	Individual Income Taxes	Corporation Income Taxes	Total Social Insurance and Retirement Receipts	Excise Taxes	Other
1962	45.7	20.6	17.1	12.6	4.0
1970	46.9	17.0	23.0	8.1	4.9
1980	47.2	12.5	30.5	4.7	5.1
1990	45.2	9.1	36.8	3.4	5.4
2000	49.6	10.2	32.2	3.4	4.5
2007	45.3	14.4	33.9	2.5	3.9
2011	47.4	7.9	35.5	3.1	6.1

Source: Compiled by author with data from U.S. Office of Management and Budget. Fiscal Year 2013 Budget of the U.S. Government: Historical Tables. February 13, 2012. http://www.white house.gov/sites/default/files/omb/budget/fy2013/assets/hist.pdf.

income. So, the shift toward more payroll tax revenues represents a shift in burden from wealthier Americans toward the middle class.

Considering carefully the budget pies, including the hidden tax expenditures piece, paints a fairly clear overall picture of what is at stake in the debate over federal deficits and debt. Concentrating on spending cuts aimed at general government operations, like reducing bureaucrats' pay, eliminating congressional earmarks, or improving efficiencies in running the national parks, will not get us very far toward reducing deficits. The non-defense discretionary spending which funds nearly everything Americans think of as "big government" (outside the military) makes up less than one-fifth of the total budget. The $646 billion spent in 2011 on non-defense discretionary spending could be eliminated entirely and still reduce only one-half of the budget deficit. The same could be said for defense spending. If Americas uniformly embraced pacifism tomorrow, a large deficit would remain. The specific programs that make up the discretionary portion of the budget pie—both the defense and the non-defense slices—also support, as we will see in detail in chapter four, essential government activities needed for America's future prosperity.

If deficit reduction is to involve cutting government spending, the hard facts of how the budget spending pie has been baked will require addressing mandatory spending. But mandatory spending includes entitlement programs millions of Americans depend upon for their incomes and to pay their medical bills. Spending cuts from these programs would be both immensely unpopular and harmful to the living standards of a large swath of American society. Nor can merely reversing some supposed recent government spending spree address the problem. Spending as a proportion of GDP, as the uptick from the stimulus spending meant to fight the Great Recession ends, remains close to where it has been for half a century. In sum, the realities presented in our budget pies show there are no painless ways to cut spending to reduce federal deficits and debt.

Public Opinion on Deficits and Debt

If the hard realities of American taxing and spending were not in themselves a barrier to addressing deficits and debt, the American public's ignorance about them compounds the difficulty. When asked what causes the federal deficit a majority of Americans cites "wasteful spending" as the reason and most think the deficit could easily be reduced through cuts in unneeded programs. But when asked about specific programs to cut, most Americans oppose cuts to most, especially the ones that dominate the budget pie. In a 2011 Gallup poll a strong majority opposed cutting Social Security, Medicare, or defense to reduce the deficit, thereby excluding from consideration fully one-half of the budget.[2] A majority agreed that cuts should come from areas other than these three. But, when provided a more specific list of possible cuts, a majority favored cutting only one: foreign aid. Many Americans seem to believe that the deficit problem can be solved through cuts to foreign aid alone. This may be because they vastly overestimate what the government spends on foreign aid, assuming it constitutes about 25 percent of federal spending. In reality, of course, foreign aid spending makes up less than 1 percent of the budget. Few Americans seem to understand much about what the federal government does or where federal spending priorities lie. Public misperception of the realities of the budget pie means most Americans have little conception of what is at stake when it comes to addressing federal deficits and debt.

Public misperception of government stems from much of the

popular rhetoric about what the federal government is about. Much of the media portrays a federal government as a bloated bureaucracy awash in waste and fraud. Of course, the federal government, given its size and complexity, sometimes does waste public money and does include some bloated bureaucracies that ought to be put on a diet. The media easily find and widely publicize anecdotes about federal bureaucrats staging lavish "conferences" in fancy resorts or poor people selling food stamps for alcohol and drugs. Less interesting for the media, however, is stories about day to day government activities that keep planes in the air, assure access to clean water, provide weather and census data essential to citizens and businesses, repair roads and bridges, or respond to emergencies. Nor do most Americans hear much about the overall shape of the budget pies as described in this chapter. As a consequence, when the issues of federal deficits and debt are raised most Americans understand little about what is at stake in the discussion. And many may be confused about how difficult addressing the problem will be.

Addendum: A Federal Budget Process Primer

Before delving into the details of taxing and spending in the next few chapters, we need a brief detour to examine the process the president and Congress use to make budgetary decisions. This detour will help the reader understand better how budget decision makers deal with the different spending categories in the budget, like discretionary and mandatory spending, and with taxes. Also, when we get to Part II, knowing the basics of this process will help the reader understand better why political confrontations over the budget have occurred when they have and how the process affects the leverage each side has in budget negotiations. The political arguments around deficits and debt usually occur in the context of the procedures and rules Congress and the president use to legislate on budgetary matters.

To understand the federal budget process, we need to delve into a little history.[3] Prior to the 1920s, there was no formal federal budget process. Federal government budgets were assembled piecemeal through congressional appropriations of funds to specific government agencies for particular programs. These appropriations were made (and are still made today) through individual appropriations bills assigning spending authority to individual federal departments and agencies. The powerful appropriations committees in the Senate and House that wrote these bills were in control of federal spending. Raising government revenues occurred separately in tax legislation written in different congressional committees—the House Ways and Means committee and the Senate Finance committee. Reflecting the constitutional assignment of the "power of the purse" to Congress, presidents played a secondary role in budgetary matters primarily through their power to veto individual appropriations and revenue bills.

During World War I, this fragmented system did not function well in managing the rapid spending increases and raising the additional revenue needed for the war. Also, budget reformers criticized the federal government's budgetary practices as not reflecting the best practices of modern business corporations in placing budgetary responsibility in the enterprise's chief executive. Both business and public administration experts advocated executive budgeting that allowed organizational spending and revenue to be managed in a coordinated manner. In response, Congress passed the Budget and Accounting Act of 1921, which, for the first time, assigned the president the responsibility of submitting an annual budget and created a Budget Bureau (now the Office of Management and Budget) to assist in the task. Now, planning for federal spending and taxation became central to the presidential job description.

The president's new budgetary powers greatly enhanced presidential power over spending and taxing. Although Congress retained the formal power of the purse—it still had to approve all appropriations and revenue legislation—the president effectively wrote the first draft of the budget from which congressional committees worked. The fragmented way Congress continued to deal with the budget through separate authorizing, appropriation, and tax bills, at least to some observers, gave the president more credibility in addressing the overall shape of the budget, particularly the size of government deficits and the growth of federal debt. As government expanded during the 1930s and 40s with the New Deal and World War II, these larger issues of the overall size of government spending, deficits, and debt became more important items on the political agenda. Yet, Congress lacked any institutional mechanisms for addressing the overall size of the budget and was forced to rely on executive branch leadership on these issues. By 1970, many in Congress feared that presidential initiative and central coordinated control over budgetary matters had diminished the venerated congressional power of the purse.

The issue came to a head in the early 1970s when the Nixon administration *impounded*, that is, refused to spend some congressionally appropriated funds. The administration claimed it had to do so to avoid adding too much to the federal deficit. Congress had no effective way to respond to this claim, since its own fragmented budgetary process did not address the overall impact of appropriations decisions on the overall size of the federal budget. In addition, Congress had to rely on the presidentially controlled Office of Management and Budget (OMB) for overall budget estimates and economic analysis. To correct this imbalance between presidential and congressional budget power, Congress passed the 1974 Congressional Budget and Impoundment Control Act (BICA). This new legislation created new budget committees in both the House and the Senate with responsibility for establishing overall levels of spending and taxing within which appropriations committees and revenue committees had to work. The budget committees were responsible for analyzing the overall size of the budget and addressing issues like overall budget deficits. Each year, the budget committees now would prepare a budget resolution determining the overall size of the budget and providing guidance to appropriations and revenue committees regarding how much could be spent and what revenue could be raised. In addition, the Act created a new Congressional Budget Office (CBO) as a counterweight to the OMB to provide Congress with an independent source of analytical advice on budgetary matters. This new congressional budget process was intended to give Congress the capacity to control the overall size of budgets and directly address deficit and debt issues.

Here is how this budget process is supposed to work as it has evolved since the 1920s: Presidents present an annual budget every January for the next federal fiscal year outlining their spending and taxing recommendations. The federal *fiscal year* is the government's annual budget year. The federal government currently budgets for a fiscal year beginning on November 1 running until the end of the following October. Fiscal years are named for the year in which they end. So, the budget the president presented in January 2013 is Budget for Fiscal Year 2014 beginning on November 1, 2013 and ending on October 31, 2014.

Once the president presents the budget, the congressional budget committees take it up and begin work on their own budget resolution which may or may not reflect the president's proposals. By April, both Houses are supposed to agree on a budget resolution that sets targets for total spending and revenues for the next fiscal year. Spending and tax committees, using the budget resolution for guidance, then work over the next few months on specific legislation which is supposed to be completed early in the summer.

Often, but not necessarily every year, the budget committees also will write a reconciliation bill that mandates certain specific changes in tax and spending laws. Unlike the budget resolution, the reconciliation bill is a statute with force of law that must be signed or vetoed by the president. Reconciliation bills have been used to mandate deficit reductions and enact tax cuts (like the Bush tax cuts in 2001 and 2003). Because, unlike any other bill, Senate rules prohibit filibusters of reconciliation bills, they have become a useful vehicle for enacting budget related measures that would not gain the sixty votes in the Senate to overcome a filibuster. (In 2010, for example, Congress enacted the tax and spending elements of Obama's Affordable Care Act in a reconciliation bill). According to the formal budget process, by October 31, all budget resolutions, tax and spending, and reconciliation bills are enacted setting the budget for the fiscal year beginning on November 1. That is the way it works on paper anyway.

The reality of budgeting since the passage of BICA of 1974 has been messier than this neat one paragraph description suggests. Political controversy over budget priorities often derails this neat process. Very often, either because of conflict within Congress itself or conflict between Congress and the president or a combination, agreement on a budget cannot be reached by the November 1 deadline. In that case, Congress must pass and the president must sign a *continuing resolution* authorizing affected departments and agencies to spend money according to the previous fiscal year's appropriation until Congress agrees on a new appropriation for the current fiscal year. Since agencies can only spend money formally appropriated by Congress, these continuing resolutions are essential for government to continue work. In some years, these continuing resolutions are passed repeatedly for many months into the new fiscal year. In recent years, as budgetary controversy and conflict has increased the situation has become enormously complicated with budgetary deadlock preventing passage of new appropriations for extended periods of time. For example, Congress was unable to agree on a budget for fiscal years 2011, 2012, or 2013 requiring continuing resolutions to keep the government running for this entire period.

Finally, another important budget process relevant to the politics of deficit and debt is the congressional debt ceiling. Before 1917, Congress had to approve every time the Treasury issued debt (i.e., sold treasury securities). During World War I, the need to borrow to fund the war effort made that impractical so Congress devised a procedure to authorize the Treasury to issue debt up to a certain dollar amount—the debt ceiling. Whenever spending obligations require Treasury to borrow more than the current ceiling, it must ask Congress to raise the debt ceiling before it can sell any more securities. Keep in mind that raising the debt ceiling, in itself, does not increase the national debt. Raising the debt ceiling only authorizes the Treasury to borrow money for debt that Congress has already incurred. In this sense, when it comes to debt, the debt ceiling is only a formality that authorizes the government to borrow to meet its obligations. Nevertheless, not raising the debt ceiling does have the real effect of preventing the Treasury from issuing debt. Being able to issue debt, however, is essential because the Treasury must sell new bonds on a continual basis to pay off old bonds as they reach their maturity dates. Like continuing resolutions, raising the debt ceiling has become a tool in the politics of deficit and debt used during times of divided government to blame the incumbent presidential administration for rising debt. And, in the summer of 2011, the Republican House of Representatives used a threat not to raise the debt limit to force the Obama administration into budget concessions.

Notes

1. Thomas L. Hungerford. "Tax Expenditures and the Federal Budget." *Congressional Research Service.* June 1, 2011 (http://www.fas.org/sgp/crs/misc/RL34622.pdf).
2. Bruce Bartlett, "Voter Ignorance Threatens Deficit Reduction," *The Fiscal Times*, February 4, 2011 (http://www.thefiscaltimes.com/Columns/2011/02/04/Voter-Ignorance-Threatens-Deficit-Reduction.aspx#page1).
3. The essential reference for all matters related to the federal budget process is: Allen Schick, *The Federal Budget: Politics, Policy, Process 3rd edition.* Washington D.C.: Brookings Institution Press, 2007.

3

DO ENTITLEMENTS ENTITLE? IS WHAT'S MANDATED MANDATORY?

Lately, there has been a lot of political talk about entitlements. Much of the talk derives from the reality that, as we saw in the last chapter, a majority of federal spending consists of mandatory spending comprised mostly of entitlement programs. If one wants to reduce future deficits through spending cuts, that means addressing entitlement spending. Yet the talk seems to go beyond technical issues connected to deficits and debt and controlling those programs that provide legally entitled benefits to beneficiaries. The term *entitlement* itself infers a moral dimension to entitlement programs, raising questions about their value irrespective of their impact on debt. We will begin our discussion of mandatory entitlement programs with reflections on this moral dimension of the notion of entitlement. We then examine in some detail components of mandatory spending—the entitlements to Social Security, Medicare, Medicaid, and other "means-tested" entitlements. Finally, we learn that because a program is a "mandatory entitlement" does not mean it cannot be changed or even eliminated—as the fate of the Aid to Families with Dependent Children (welfare) proved.

Entitlement

The moral connotations we associate with "entitlement" are those we traditionally associate with the classic spoiled rich kid who thinks her/his exalted status demands special privileges greater than what are available to ordinary people. This moral connotation focuses on an understanding of the word as a "sense of entitlement" or "an entitlement mentality."

The entitled rich are those who enjoy the attributes of a plush existence—manicured neighborhoods, opulent houses, access to prestigious schools, private jets, etc.—irrespective of moral character, hard work, or individual achievement. Today, however, for some, the targets of moral condemnations of an entitlement mentality are not the undeserving rich, but the far from rich beneficiaries of government programs. The use of the technical, legal term *entitlement* to refer to benefits given to individuals because they are legally entitled to receive them has opened the door to evaluating these benefits with the connotation of the conventional moral understanding of the term. Entitled beneficiaries are portrayed as grasping individuals lacking personal responsibility and who demand government support for their needs irrespective of whether they deserve them. At times from this perspective, entitlement programs are portrayed as giving special privileges to particular classes of individuals that are denied to ordinary citizens and at their expense. At other times, society as a whole is portrayed as infected with an entitlement mentality that leads vast numbers of Americans to demand government benefits rather than meet their needs through individual effort.

The moral condemnation of entitlement mentality has become a significant element in the politics of deficits and debt. To the extent that the entitlement spending is seen as essentially income transfers from hardworking responsible taxpayers to undeserving entitled beneficiaries, these programs become more acceptable targets for cuts. Even when large numbers of Americans benefit from entitlement programs (think Social Security or Medicare), the concept of entitlement mentality serves to justify cutbacks in these programs in the name of promoting more personal responsibility. This view of entitlement divides society into givers (taxpayers) who pay for the benefits of takers (the entitled) who get government support. Amid fears of growing deficits and debt, reducing undeserved entitlements comes to be seen as reducing privileges of the specially entitled groups on behalf of a broader public interest in reducing debt.

This view of entitlements contrasts dramatically with an older conception that views entitlement programs like Social Security, Medicare, or Food Stamps as fundamental expressions of our common welfare. Rather than undermining the public interest, these social benefits were an expression of a mutual commitment that no individual would be left to suffer from life's adversity alone. Social benefits did not divide citizens into givers and takers but united people in solidarity to support each other in times of need. The programs that make up mandatory spending were not born as efforts to entitle particular groups, but as *social insurance* against misfortunes that might befall anyone. Understanding this older conception of social insurance is critical if citizens are to make wise choices about the place entitlement spending should have in reducing deficits and debt.

The entitlement programs that comprise the majority of federal spending are all the children of the New Deal. They first emerged as a response to the economic calamity that was the Great Depression. The stock market collapse of 1929 and the ensuing banking crisis destroyed the savings, incomes, and basic economic security of millions of Americans. By 1933, 25 percent of Americans were unemployed; those with jobs endured devastating declines in wages, and millions saw their life savings vanish as banks collapsed across the country. When he came into office in 1932, President Franklin D. Roosevelt pledged to respond to the crisis with his New Deal for the American people. Initially, New Deal programs focused on stemming the banking crisis and providing immediate relief to destitute Americans, but FDR soon turned his attention to creating a permanent institutional framework to provide Americans with economic security. In 1934, he appointed a Committee on Economic Security that drafted the legislation which became the Social Security Act of 1935—the foundation of America's system of unemployment compensation, the Social Security program—from which Medicare and the country's safety net programs for the poor evolved.

The authors of the Social Security Act viewed it as social insurance against the risks of not being able to earn an income in a capitalist market society. In a market society, most individuals, most of the time, are expected to earn income for themselves and their families through earning wages or profits from a business. Yet everyone faces the risk of circumstances such as unemployment, ill health, a permanent disability, or exhaustion of savings in old age, which conceivably would make earning an income impossible. FDR called these risks the "hazards and vicissitudes of life" from which no one is immune. To protect against these risks, social insurance spreads these risks across the entire citizenry just as say, fire insurance spreads the risk of a fire among the pool of all those who buy fire insurance. Social insurance programs mandate that citizens contribute (usually in the form of taxes) to generate sufficient revenue to provide for individuals in times of need. Just as not everyone who pays fire insurance premiums experiences a fire and collects on the insurance, citizens who pay taxes to support social programs do not all derive the same benefit from the program. But because individuals cannot predict with certainty whether they might lose their ability to earn a living in the marketplace due to unforeseeable circumstances, all are served by contributing to the system, although some individuals ultimately will receive more benefits from the system than others. Social insurance shifts the risk of the "hazards and vicissitudes of life" from the individual's shoulders to all of society. Entitlement programs such as social insurance are not special privileges that the government bestows on particular classes of individuals but universal benefits drawn on as needed.

Critics of social insurance argue that it relieves individuals of the personal responsibility to protect themselves from life's adverse events through the purchase of private insurance or savings. While not denying that individuals ought to prudently save and purchase insurance to protect themselves from misfortune, social insurance proponents make two arguments for the need for the added protection of pooled risks against misfortune. First, due to the reality of economic inequality, many workers have limited capacity to save and protect themselves from adversity. Someone earning a low income and with little savings, if unemployed, will quickly exhaust those savings, so unemployment insurance can be essential for survival. The pooling of contributions in social insurance programs compensate for the unequal distribution of the capacity to save in the marketplace. Second, even for those with a greater capacity to save, a catastrophic loss can quickly exhaust even a large pool of savings. For example, no one, even the most prudent saver, is immune from the huge medical bills that often result from illness. Individuals cannot know when such a disaster might strike them and few would be financially prepared alone to pay for it. Insurance allows spreading the risk of catastrophe among a large pool of individuals so that the resources of all can be drawn on to take care of the misfortunes of the few.

Two of the programs created in the Social Security Act clearly reflected this social insurance model. First, the unemployment compensation program mandated that states establish unemployment insurance funds drawing on contributions from employers. Workers laid off from their jobs receive unemployment compensation checks from these funds for a limited period of time until they find other work. The state funds are intended to provide assistance in normal economic times for short periods of unemployment. In times of recession, when the number of unemployed increase and there is more long term unemployment, the state unemployment compensation funds receive infusions of revenue from the federal treasury. Second, the Social Security program established a system based on participating workers contributing to the program through payroll taxes and thereby qualifying to receive benefits. Initially, Social Security was meant to provide only benefits upon retirement, but by the 1950s, the program was expanded to include disability benefits and survivors' benefits to the spouse and children of a qualified worker. The creation of Medicare in 1965 supplemented Social Security with health insurance for the elderly financed through an addition to the payroll tax. As we have seen, Social Security and Medicare have become the largest of the entitlement programs constituting the bulk of the mandatory spending in the budget.

The Social Security Act also created some federally funded entitlements that deviated from a strict social insurance model. It established the basis for the current safety net for the poor in public assistance payments to destitute mothers with children (a program soon to be known as "welfare"), the blind, and the elderly not qualified for Social Security. These programs drew on general tax revenues to fund their benefits rather than on social insurance contributions. Nevertheless, the logic of social insurance could be applied to these benefits for the poor as well. All of us and our family members, this logic argues, are subject to the risk of falling into poverty. In paying our taxes to support programs for the poor, we, in effect, are creating a political commitment that assures that none of us will be abandoned in times of dire need. Considered in this larger sense of the mutual obligations all citizens owe to one another in a common society, those entitlements that comprise the safety net for the poor also embrace the overall logic of social insurance.

Social Security

Social Security has become America's largest and most expensive federal program. While we associate the program with retirement benefits paid to senior citizens, it also provides substantial income support to non-elderly Americans who receive disability or survivors benefits. In 2011, $727 billion in Social Security spending provided payments to 55 million Americans, about 16 percent of the total population. Of these, 38 million were retirees and their dependents, a little over 10 million disabled workers and their dependents, and around 6 million survivors. Elderly Americans overall depend on Social Security for about 41 percent of their income. That percentage understates, however, the importance of the program to the incomes of large subsets of seniors. Fifty-four percent of all married couples depend on the program for over 50 percent of their income and for 22 percent it provides 90 percent of their income. Unmarried seniors, who tend to be less economically secure, are much more dependent on their Social Security checks: 73 percent depend on it for 50 percent of income and 43 percent for 90 percent of income. Understandably, given these percentages, without Social Security, a very large percent of elderly Americans would live in severe poverty. At present, only 14 percent of seniors have incomes below the poverty line; without Social Security, over 50 percent would be in poverty. No wonder, then, that Social Security has been such a popular program and one most Americans support.

One also can project that Social Security will be important to the economic security of millions of Americans in the future. At present, nearly 95 percent of the current work force is covered by Social Security and anticipates receiving benefits at retirement. Perhaps to a greater extent than current retirees, those in the future will depend more on the program because of declines in private pension coverage. Right now only about 50 percent of workers have any pension coverage at all and that percentage has been declining. Moreover, many of those pensions have been cut back as corporations and state and local governments have faced fiscal pressure and because of poor investment performance. Most pensions nowadays are 401K "defined contribution" pensions whose returns depend on individual workers' skills in managing their own retirement investments, and they have not been managed well. Most evidence suggests that even those with pensions cannot expect them to provide much retirement income. These realities mean that the standard of living of elderly Americans in the future depends greatly on the fiscal health of the Social Security program. Will adequate Social Security benefits be there for future retirees?

Answering this question requires an excursion into the history of Social Security financing. When first created in 1935, Social Security policy makers envisioned workers paying into a Social Security Trust fund that would steadily accumulate assets from which benefits would be paid—payroll taxes would begin immediately, and the first benefit payments were scheduled in the next decade. When taxes first began to be collected in 1936, however, politicians on both the left and right objected to the quickly ballooning Trust fund. Those on the left were concerned that the taxes were depressing economic performance (and most economists now attribute the 1937 recession partly to the imposition of Social Security taxes); those on the right worried that the federal government was in control of such a large pool of potential investment revenue. Would Social Security administrators invest in the stock market potentially giving the government financial control of the private economy? Would the Social Security Trust fund lead to socialism?

To allay these concerns, Congress voted in 1939 to change the financing of Social Security to a "pay as you go" system. Rather than accumulate reserves in the Trust fund, current Social Security tax revenues would be paid out immediately to beneficiaries. In the early years, the favorable ratio of workers paying tax to eligible beneficiaries (15:1 in 1950) meant that even very low tax rates provided more than enough revenue to meet the program's needs. In response to this abundance, Congress added survivors and the disabled as eligible beneficiaries and steadily increased the generosity of benefits in the fifties and sixties. Through these decades, Congress was able to repeatedly increase Social Security benefit levels with only small, nearly unnoticeable increases in the payroll tax. By the late 1970s, however, this happy fiscal situation came to an end and a Social Security crisis waited around the corner.

The problem was the passage of time. By the 1970s, many more Social Security eligible retirees were receiving checks. The large ratios of paying workers to beneficiaries had declined steadily during the previous twenty years. In 1975 there were now only 3.2 workers for each beneficiary. Also, Congress had boosted benefits substantially in the 1960s to reduce poverty among the elderly, which worked, but increased program costs. Projections now showed that around 1983, Social Security would not collect enough revenue to pay projected benefits. Also, actuaries began pointing out the retirement of the baby boom generation that had just entered the workforce and its impact on finances over the long run.

To address this crisis, congressional leaders and President Reagan appointed a commission led by economist and later Federal Reserve Board Chair Alan Greenspan to come up with a solution. In 1983, the Greenspan Commission recommended and Congress enacted a major reform in Social Security financing. To solve the immediate crisis, Social Security taxes were raised substantially and increases were to continue gradually in the coming years. In addition, the future retirement age of the baby boomers would be increased gradually from sixty-five to sixty-seven. These changes now provided more than enough revenue to fund benefits on the pay as you go basis, allowing the excess to begin to accumulate in the Trust fund in order to cover the future cost of retiring baby boomers. To allay any fear that fund revenues would be invested in the private economy, the Greenspan reform provided for the Trust fund to be invested solely in U.S. Treasury securities. In effect, Social Security would help fund the national debt, creating a major portion of the intragovermental portion of the debt described in chapter 1.

The first boomers began to retire in 2011 and soon (about 2014), Social Security will begin drawing down the Trust fund to cover the added costs of their benefits. (Social Security administrators actually had to briefly draw from the fund in 2010 to cover a shortfall in payroll taxes resulting from the recession.) The Congressional Budget Office estimates that the baby boom generation will cause the percentage of Americans over sixty-five to rise from 21 percent of the population in 2010 to 36 percent by 2035. The total cost of Social Security will rise from 4.9 percent of GDP in 2010 to 6.1 percent in 2035. These added costs mean that Social Security finances will be stressed. Current projections from the Social Security Trustees show the savings in the Trust fund running out around 2036. At that point, Social Security once more will be on a strictly pay as you go basis and projections show revenues at that time adequate to cover only about 75 percent of projected benefits. What is to be done?

These projections, widely covered in the media, have generated much alarmist rhetoric about Social Security. Words like "crisis," "bankruptcy," and "insolvency" have been used to describe the situation and these reports have raised the specter that Social Security will fail to deliver retirement benefits to future generations. In reality, as we have seen, Social Security, even when the Trust fund is exhausted, under current policies, will generate enough revenue to meet three-quarters of projected obligations. Rather than a crisis, Social Security has a future fiscal *problem*, but one prudent policy changes can correct and place program finances on a firm basis far into the century. Growing Social Security costs also are a factor in the overall growth of the national debt, but not the major contributor to that growth.

Bringing Social Security into *actuarial balance*—earning sufficient revenues to pay all benefits—far into the future would not require any major changes to the program. In a 2010 report, the Congressional Budget Office analyzed the impact on future actuarial balance of thirty relatively minor changes, such as small increases in the Social Security tax, changes in the benefit formula, increases in the retirement age, or small reductions in cost of living increases.[1] The report shows that adopting only two or three of these options would solve Social Security's financial problem.

For example, various options that increase the amount of income subject to the Social Security tax could have a large impact on future revenues. Since its inception, the Social Security tax has been applied only to earnings up to a certain amount—the taxable maximum. The 1983 reforms provided for this maximum to rise gradually according to a formula linked to the increase in average wages. (The taxable maximum was $106,800 in 2010.) In 1983, the taxable maximum subjected about 90 percent of all income earned to this tax, but because the incomes of the highest income earners have increased faster than average earnings since 1983, the proportion of total earnings subject to tax has dropped to 83 percent. Simply recalibrating the formula to assure that it was high enough to once again capture 90 percent of earnings would, by itself, extend the life of the Trust fund eleven years until 2050. If the taxable maximum were eliminated entirely, that is, if 100 percent of income were subject to tax, the Trust fund will last until 2083. Because raising the taxable maximum, under the current benefit formula, also would result in some increase in benefit payments for higher income workers, one could have a greater impact on Social Security's finances if the taxable maximum were increased without increasing benefits. If the taxable maximums were eliminated and the benefit formula changed to not increase benefits, the Trust fund would never be exhausted—problem solved!

Of course, it is unlikely that Congress would ever adopt a single change to address the problem. But a combination of small changes such as restoring coverage of the taxable maximum to 90 percent of funding, some small reduction in payments to high income recipients, raising the retirement age a year or two, or a 1 percent increase in tax would make Social Security solvent for the foreseeable future. So making the program financially secure is not a difficult problem. In addition, raising more revenue or trimming future benefits in Social Security also would reduce the program's overall contribution to the national debt as a whole.

Even though Social Security reform might contribute to easing the overall debt, the fact that the Social Security Trust fund is invested in U.S. Treasuries has additional implications for the larger national debt. While the Trust fund is an asset to the Social Security program, it is a future liability to the federal government as a whole. When Social Security must cash in its Treasury bonds to pay beneficiaries, the Treasury will have to come up with the funds to meet this obligation. This fact leads some to claim that the bonds in the Trust fund are nothing but worthless IOUs instead of "real" assets that can fund future program obligations. These critics claim the contributions to the fund already have been "spent" since they were loaned to support government spending since 1983.

There are two flaws with this line of argument. First, federal government obligations to the Trust fund are the same as to anyone who owns Treasury bonds. The government cannot renege on redeeming Trust fund bonds without calling into question the entire faith and credit of the United States. If this happened, the Treasury would not be able to find anyone willing to purchase Treasury bonds, except, perhaps, at exorbitant interest rates. Only if there were a genuine fiscal crisis due to a debt so large that the federal government was forced to renege on the entire debt could one imagine a failure to meet Social Security Trust fund obligations. In such a monumental fiscal, economic, and, inevitably, political crisis, the solvency of Social Security would be the least of the nation's concerns. Second, even though excess Social Security taxes since 1983 have been loaned to the federal government that does not mean they have been spent and are not real assets to the program.

Bonds in the fund have replaced borrowing that otherwise would have occurred from private investors to meet federal spending obligations and, consequently, they have served to reduce government interest payments on the publically held debt. The Trust fund bonds remain legal obligations that the federal government must pay.

Nevertheless, the impact on American society of meeting Social Security Trust fund obligations will depend on the level of overall debt as the program draws on the fund to pay benefits. If the overall debt situation is stable and the Treasury can find lenders willing to purchase new Treasury bonds at the same or lower interest rate than it paid for the Trust fund bonds, it simply will roll over the fund bonds into new bonds sold to new investors. In this scenario, the overall debt would remain the same; only the owners of the debt would change. High and growing levels of debt in the future, however, would make matters more difficult. The federal government might have to pay high interest rates to roll over Trust fund debt, requiring imposing higher taxes or reducing spending on other programs as a result. Meeting future Social Security obligations in this scenario would place burdens on future generations even if the program were technically solvent. Social Security's future burden, then, is connected directly to the nation's future fiscal condition.

Medicare and Medicaid

Both Medicare and Medicaid can be thought of as daughters of the New Deal, even though they were enacted thirty years later. Roosevelt's 1935 Committee on Economic Security had proposed universal health insurance as a part of its overall social insurance plan, but FDR opted not to include it in the Social Security Act. He was concerned that certain opposition to health insurance from the politically powerful American Medical Association might undermine the entire legislative package. Social insurance advocates, however, continued to view the cost of illness as a key economic risk that any comprehensive social insurance system should cover. In Europe, for example, some form of universal health insurance was at the core of its social insurance systems and proved extremely popular with its citizens. In 1948, President Truman proposed adding universal health insurance to the Social Security framework, only to see his proposal defeated in

Congress amid an intense propaganda campaign from opponents who labeled his proposal "socialized medicine." After the failure of Truman's effort, over the next fifteen years, liberal proponents of health insurance concentrated their efforts on enacting health insurance coverage for the segment of the population most vulnerable to the costs of illness—the elderly. This effort finally bore fruit with the passage of the largest expansion of social insurance since the 1930s when President Lyndon B. Johnson signed the Social Security Amendments of 1965 establishing Medicare, universal health insurance for Americans over age 65, and Medicaid, health insurance for the poor.

The focus on the insurance needs of the elderly complemented the shape of America's health care system as it was evolving in the 1950s. By the middle of that decade, a majority of American workers received health insurance as a fringe benefit from their employers. America's unique employment-based health insurance system emerged during WWII when wage and price controls limited the ability of employers to offer higher wages to attract good workers. Instead, they offered attractive fringe benefits like health insurance. Also, in the absence of a government-run universal health insurance system, labor unions made the demand for health insurance a standard demand in labor management negotiations.

The federal government encouraged the growth of this employer based system through the tax code with enactment, in 1954, of legislation that exempted employee health insurance benefits from taxation and allowed businesses to deduct their contributions to health insurance premiums. With these tax benefits in place, by the mid-1950s most employees could expect health insurance coverage as a standard employment benefit. By this time, a sizable private health insurance industry had developed, including both non-profit community health insurers like Blue Cross/Blue Shield and for-profit insurers who wrote the employer-based policies.

Of course, millions of Americans were left outside this system either because they were self-employed, worked for employers who did not offer insurance, or did not work. Some without employer-based coverage purchased expensive insurance in the individual market, but most simply were uncovered. Among this latter group were most elderly retirees. Prior to Medicare, health insurance simply was not available for most elderly Americans. Upon retirement, most lost their employer-based insurance and private individual insurance was unaffordable as well. The high risk of insuring older people who were likely to develop health problems meant insurers were not eager to enroll them except in return for very high premiums.

Medicare, then, met a genuine social need in giving millions of seniors access to health care. The program covers hospital costs (Part A), the most expensive item most beneficiaries face, offers medical insurance to cover doctor's visits and other medical costs (Part B) for a small premium, and since 2004, drug coverage (Part D). Since its inception, Medicare has been seen as an extension of Social Security. Not only do beneficiaries enroll in both programs at about the same time in their lives, upon retirement, but direct links exist between the programs as seen in automatic deductions of Medicare Part B premiums from social security checks. Moreover, Medicare is financed, like Social Security, through a payroll tax deduction. Like Social Security, workers' Medicare tax contributions qualify them to receive the program's benefits when they reach the age of eligibility. The creation of Medicare provided a significant addition, beyond Social Security, to the economic security of the elderly.

Medicaid serves a population that the employer-based private insurance system would never cover—the indigent poor.[2] Like Medicare, Medicaid descends from the 1935 Social Security Act as an extension of the public assistance titles of that legislation. And like most of these safety net programs, Medicaid, in contrast to the entirely federally funded Medicare program, is jointly funded and administered by the states. States currently cover about 43 percent, on average, of Medicaid costs nationwide—yet the precise percentage varies widely from state to state.

The federal government sets minimum eligibility levels, but states may opt to exceed those minimum levels and receive federal matching funds for that enhanced coverage. States must cover families with children living below the official federal poverty line, but are not required to cover non-elderly childless adults, although eight states do. States also must cover indigent elderly and disabled adults—those who are eligible for federally funded public assistance (SSI). Since 1997, states also receive a block grant (the CHIP program) to cover uninsured children in families earning up to two and one-half the poverty level.

Because of state discretion in determining eligibility, who is or is not covered varies widely across the country. However, nationwide a majority of Medicaid recipients are children and their parents while about 25 percent are elderly or disabled. However, although they make up a minority of recipients, the elderly and disabled account for two-thirds of Medicaid costs because of the high cost of nursing home and long-term care. Because Medicare does not cover long-term care, many elderly and disabled people become eligible for Medicaid when they exhaust their savings by paying for such care. Medicaid accounts for about 50 percent of the cost of nursing home care nationally.

Medicaid and Medicare were negligible parts of the federal budget when first created in the 1960s. Now combined, they are the largest single expenditure item—$856 billion in 2011. Most of this, about $560 billion, is for Medicare (see Figure 3.1). These high costs are a reflection, in part, of the importance of these programs in providing so many Americans access to health care. Medicare insures about 50 million elderly Americans and Medicaid covers around 55 million people, together providing health coverage to one-third of the population. But future projections show health care spending growing exponentially as a proportion of the budget over the next few decades. According to the Congressional Budget Office (CBO), health care spending in the federal budget will double by 2037 from about 5.6 percent of GDP now to 9.6 to 10.4 percent.[3] In fact, as we will see in chapter 6, some projections show increasing health care spending as the primary factor in growing debt in the future.

Why has health care spending become such a large component of the federal budget and why is it projected to rise so much in coming decades? One big part of the answer is the aging population.[4] More people have become eligible for the Medicare entitlement in recent decades and, with the baby boomer retirements, many more will do so in the future. The costs of insuring older people inevitably will be high because they are the most likely to need high cost care to treat chronic diseases, such as diabetes, asthma, and heart disease, and it is also expensive to treat conditions like cancer to which the elderly are more vulnerable. An aging population also boosts Medicaid spending because so much of its budget goes to long-term nursing home care. Through about 2037, which spans the era of baby boom retirees,

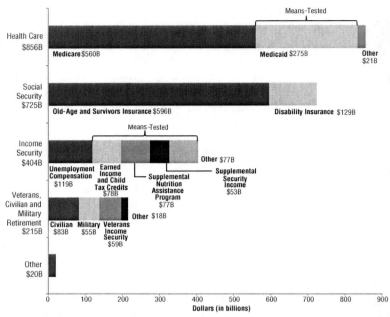

Source: Based on chart from Congressional Budget Office. "The U.S. Federal Budget: A Closer Look at Mandatory Spending." April 17, 2010. http://cbo.gov/sites/default/files/cbofiles/attachments/BS_Mandatory_print.pdf

Figure 3.1   Mandatory Spending in 2011

aging alone, according to the CBO, will account for about half of the increase in health care spending in the budget.

The other half comes from increasing per capita costs of providing health services to individual health care beneficiaries. Rising federal health care spending reflects the overall growth in health care costs in the economy, which have grown, on average, 2.4 times the rate of inflation since 1970. Most analysts attribute much of the rising costs to new medical technology, including new drug therapies that successfully treat a wider range of diseases. Fifty years ago, treatments that we now take for granted, such as open heart surgery and cancer chemotherapy did not exist; their success in treating disease has added to the cost of health care. These new technologies also allow people to live longer, sometimes with chronic conditions that require monitoring and further treatment. Future improvements in health technology also can be counted on to add to costs. More expensive health care seems to follow naturally from growing affluence. All of us understand the value of being healthy and, as medical science offers new ways to help us achieve good health, we are willing to pay to have it. Devoting more societal resources, including public ones, to health care seems to be a consequence of growing prosperity.

Many health care experts also argue that the system for delivering care encourages overutilization of medical services without necessarily improving health outcomes. Most health care providers are paid on a fee-for service basis which means that they are compensated for every procedure they provide. Since in most cases insurance pays the cost of treatment, the cost of a procedure deters neither the provider nor the patient from opting for it. This structure of incentives for both the provider, who only gets paid if a service is provided, and the patient, who does not have to bear the cost of the service, leads them to opt for medical procedures even if unnecessary. Critics claim that these perverse incentives add costs throughout the system from patients who run to the doctor at the first sign of a sniffle, to physicians, who recommend orthopedic surgery for leg pain when physical therapy would be just as effective. Given these incentives, the growth of insurance coverage itself and the decline of patient out-of-pocket payments for health service, which declined from 40 percent of health expenditures in 1970 to 14 percent in 2010, have led to higher health costs. Beyond the flawed system incentives, health system critics also cite the fragmented nature of the system, which separates primary care physicians from specialists, prevents identifying appropriate treatments efficiently.

The passage of the Affordable Care Act (ACA, also known as "Obamacare") in 2009 expanded the federal government's responsibility for financing the health care of Americans, although its impact on future debt is uncertain. Unlike Medicare and Medicaid, the ACA did not create a new entitlement. Instead, the legislation created a mechanism to expand access to private health insurance in two ways: first, states were mandated to raise the eligibility for Medicaid to all individuals and families earning up to 133 percent of the poverty level—with the federal government paying for most of the increased cost. (The Supreme Court eventually declared this mandate unconstitutional allowing state governments to reject the federal funds and not expand eligibility—an option about half the states chose as of 2013.) Second, insurance exchanges would be established in each state through which currently uninsured people could buy health insurance. The law included an individual mandate to buy insurance (upheld by the Supreme Court) or face a modest fine. This controversial requirement was seen as essential to assure that the total pool of insured included healthy people as well as those needing health care and prevent individuals from becoming "free riders"—refusing to buy insurance until they were sick. The federal government will subsidize the purchase of insurance for low income people.

While the Medicaid expansion and insurance subsidies will add to federal spending, ACA advocates argued that the legislation would lead to slower increases in system wide health costs in the future, thereby reducing long-term federal health care costs. Providing increased access to health insurance is supposed to keep individuals from seeking expensive care in emergency rooms and to encourage preventative care that reduces eventual expensive treatments for chronic conditions. Also, the legislation provided for ways to encourage reform in the health care delivery system. (Some of these reforms will be examined in chapter 10.) Whether or not the ACA increases or decreases future debt will depend on whether it succeeds in reducing rising costs in the overall health system. Some remain skeptical, suggesting that these efforts will fail and that the ACA eventually will only add to federal health care costs.

Because growing health care spending looms so large as a part of the future national debt problem, reforming the health care system to make it more efficient has been central to the conversation. Nevertheless, even if system reform could slow the growth of health care costs, those costs are still likely to rise in the future. The aging of the population and the expenses of future health technology will make the system more costly no matter how efficient it might become. Any effort to reduce future deficits and debt needs to factor in rising health costs as a given.

Means-Tested Entitlements

About two-thirds of mandatory spending in the federal budget supports the two largest entitlement programs we have just discussed, Medicare and Social Security. Of the remaining third, about 20 percent of mandatory spending ($404 billion in 2011) goes to a variety of income support programs (see Figure 3.1). For example, unemployment compensation, the largest of these, totaled $119 billion in 2011. Medicare, Social Security, and unemployment compensation are universal entitlements available to eligible recipient regardless of income. They often are considered "middle-class" entitlements because they provide support to the vast majority of Americans at some point in their lives.

A much smaller portion of mandatory spending is devoted to means-tested entitlements for the poor. In 2011, the federal government spent about $566 billion on means-tested programs, including Medicaid, which constituted $275 billion or roughly half this amount. Although critics of government entitlement spending often focus on these programs for the poor when warning of rising entitlement spending, they make up only one-fourth of all entitlements. And if we subtract Medicaid, only 15 percent of entitlement spending goes to support the incomes of the poor.

A wide variety of programs fit into the category of means-tested income support entitlements. The two largest programs are the Earned Income Tax Credit (EITC) program and Food Stamps. EITC supplements the incomes of the working poor—those working either full or part time but earning extremely low incomes. To receive EITC, a worker must file a tax return documenting all income earned; those earning below a certain amount receive payments from the government (EITC will be described in more detail in chapter 5.) The Supplemental Nutritional Assistance Program (SNAP), popularly known as Food Stamps, provides income support to low income Americans to be spent on food. EITC and SNAP combined account for over half of means-tested income support ($155 billion in 2011). Another $53 billion goes for the Supplemental Security Income (SSI) program that provides cash payments to poor elderly and disabled people who do not qualify for Social Security, usually because their work histories did not qualify them. The balance of the means-tested safety net consists of a variety of programs for energy assistance, nutritional supplements for pregnant women, housing assistance, etc.

In addition to these middle-class and means-tested entitlements, the balance of mandatory spending goes to support federal civilian and military retirement, veterans' programs, and a variety of other minor programs.

Entitlements Can Be Ended: The Case of Welfare

Words like *mandatory* and *entitlement* may imply an unwarranted permanence to this spending. Congress can, after all, modify or eliminate these programs whenever it chooses. Even so, the aura of permanence and immutability often associated with entitlements or mandatory spending derives primarily from the political popularity of the two biggest programs: Social Security and Medicare. Any attempt to address future deficits through reduction or modification of benefits in either program will produce solid resistance from the senior citizens who currently benefit and existing workers who anticipate receiving the same benefits when they retire. These entitlements would be difficult to modify, not because of their technical status as "mandatory spending" programs, but because of their strong political constituencies. Without such strong political support, however, entitlements can be withdrawn. A case in point is the fate of one of the oldest entitlements of them all, included in the 1935 Social Security Act, the entitlement to welfare.

The Aid to Dependent Children program (later Aid to *Families* with Dependent Children – AFDC) was among the original public assistance entitlements included in the social security legislation. The program was intended to provide cash assistance to mothers with children who had no source of income. The original legislative authors clearly imagined these mothers to be widows who had lost a breadwinning husband. With the addition of the survivors' benefit to Social Security in the 1940s, there was an expectation that need for the program would wither away since most widows would be eligible for benefits under that program as Social Security coverage expanded.

By the 1950s, however, it was clear that AFDC was not going to wither away. Rather than being a program that assisted primarily widows, a group many would deem the deserving poor, most welfare recipients were unmarried women who had born their children out of wedlock. As the perception of welfare as a program for needy widows was replaced with one of women with "dubious moral character," it became an easy target for citizens angered over taxes supporting undeserving people and politicians willing to exploit those perceptions. That a substantial proportion of welfare recipients, by the 1960s, were African-American also gave a racial aspect to white attitudes toward the program.

By the 1980s, the general public hostility toward AFDC took on an added dimension when conservative writers elaborated a systematic critique of the program around the concept of dependency. Because young women became eligible for the welfare entitlement by having a child, these writers argued that welfare encouraged out-of-wedlock births. Pointing to rising rates of illegitimacy among young, particularly African-American women, they claimed that AFDC created perverse incentives that led poor women to have children to obtain welfare benefits rather than engage in more constructive behavior, such as staying in school or seeking job skills. With welfare cash available, these critics argued, these women had little incentive to marry or develop stable relationships with men and men had little need to take responsibility for the support of their children.

For program critics, welfare created a culture of dependency in which poor women came to depend on welfare for their livelihood rather that pursuing opportunities to gain employment or improve their incomes. This culture was passed from generation to generation, according to this argument, creating a permanent underclass dependent on the welfare system. Because welfare also provided very meager incomes to recipients, it also perpetuated rather than alleviated poverty. For its critics, rather than a benefit for poor mothers, welfare was a trap that kept them in poverty. Even though many social science studies of the actual experience of welfare recipients found little support for the theory of cultural dependence, it resonated with the public, media commentators, and politicians. By the 1990s, many Republican and Democratic elected officials came to believe that welfare dependency required a radical change in AFDC.

In 1996, a Republican Congress enacted and a Democratic President, Bill Clinton, signed legislation to end the welfare entitlement. AFDC was abolished and replaced with the Temporary Assistance to Needy Families program (TANF). Rather than providing all poor mothers with children with a federal entitlement to cash assistance, TANF gave states a block grant of funds equivalent to what the state had previously received—through AFDC—to pay welfare cash benefits. Under the new legislation, states were not obligated to provide assistance to all poor mothers in the state—there was no longer an entitlement to assistance. Rather, states were allowed to limit how many poor mothers received assistance and TANF mandated that all recipients work. States also were encouraged to spend portions of their TANF block grant on things other than cash assistance, such as job training programs, child care, or organizing work programs for recipients.

TANF also was time limited, with no one allowed to receive cash benefits for periods longer than three years and no more than five years in a lifetime. States were free to impose shorter time limits if they wished. With the end of the welfare entitlement, welfare rolls plummeted. Part of the decline was a consequence of a booming economy in the late 1990s that created more job opportunities even for former welfare recipients, but much of the decline was the consequence of tighter state eligibility rules and other state policies designed to limit access. Many pointed to dropping welfare rolls as evidence of TANF's success, but continued high poverty rates suggested to some observers that the welfare entitlement's demise simply had increased economic insecurity among the poor.

From the standpoint of entitlements and their relation to policies to reduce future deficits and debt, the TANF experience does show that entitlements are not permanent. Policy makers may turn to reducing entitlement spending or even eliminating entitlements to bring down debt. The experience also suggests that which entitlements get reduced may relate to the political clout of whom they entitle. Mean-tested entitlements targeted at the poor obviously are politically more vulnerable than the middle-class entitlements. Yet this also poses a dilemma for debt reduction. Means-tested entitlements comprise only a relatively small proportion of overall mandatory spending. Even if major cuts were made to means-tested entitlements, there would be little impact on future debt. For mandatory spending cuts to have a major role in controlling future deficit and debt, the popular middle-class entitlements like Social Security and Medicare would have to be on the table.

Notes

1. Congressional Budget Office, *Social Security Policy Options,* July 1, 2010 (http://www.cbo.gov/publication/21547).
2. A terrific source for data on Medicare, Medicaid, and health care policy generally is the Kaiser Family Foundation (http://www.kff.org/); Medicaid Data can be found at http://www.kff.org/medicaid/8162.cfm.
3. Congressional Budget Office, *The 2012 Long-Term Budget Outlook,* June 5, 2012 (http://www.cbo.gov/publication/43288), 48.
4. Kaiser Family Foundation, "Health Care Costs: A Primer," May 9, 2012 (http://www.kff.org/insurance/7670.cfm).

4

HOW DISCRETIONARY IS DISCRETIONARY SPENDING?

As we saw in the previous chapter, *mandatory* and *entitlement* are words with both a technical meaning and political connotations. We also saw that programs that have these adjectives attached to them are nevertheless subject to change and even elimination, depending on the political circumstances. In this chapter, we apply a similar examination to the idea of *discretionary* spending. We begin with a discussion of what the term *discretionary spending* really means technically, and then go on to provide some historical background, and then discuss defense and non-defense spending in this context. We conclude by looking at the possible future budgetary impact of programs in the discretionary spending category.

Discretionary Spending?

When asked the best synonym for the word *discretionary*, a thesaurus gives the word *optional*. This connotation might lead someone untutored in the jargon of the federal budget to assume that spending in this category must be "optional" and not central to the task of governing. In fact, the slightly over one-third of the federal budget labeled discretionary funds the core functions of our government. This spending pays for most of the government activity dedicated, as the Constitution's preamble eloquently puts it, "to establish Justice, insure domestic Tranquility, provide for the common defense, promote the General Welfare, and secure the Blessings of Liberty...."

Most of what most Americans think of when they think of the federal government falls into the category of discretionary spending. This expenditure pays for the salaries of all federal bureaucrats, funds our troops overseas and at home, finances the entire federal judiciary—as well as all federal law enforcement—supports scientific and health research, regulates the health and safety of Americans, provides federal grants to state and local governments, build roads, bridges, and dams across the country, and the myriad of other activities for which the federal government has responsibility. All the government departments and agencies with their well-known acronyms like NASA, FDA, CDC, ATF, FBI, FCC, FTC, SEC, et al. fall within the category of discretionary spending as do all the armed services. In short, a look at what is included in the budgetary category *discretionary* spending shows clearly that it actually is not entirely *optional*. There is relatively little that is discretionary in discretionary spending. (Figures 4.1 and 4.2 show the relative size of non-defense and defense discretionary spending and the major categories within each.)

As we saw in chapter 2, the designation of this spending as discretionary is meant to contrast it with the mandatory spending of the major entitlement programs like Social Security, Medicare, and Medicaid. It is discretionary only in the sense that Congress can modify this spending in the annual budget appropriation process, unlike the

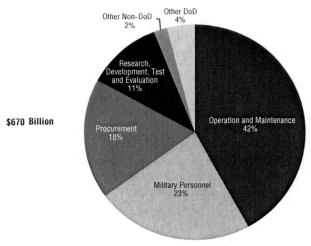

Source: Compiled by author with data from Elmendorf, Douglas W. and the Congressional Budget Office. "Choices for Federal Spending and Taxes." September 17, 2012. http://www.cbo.gov/publication/43619?utm_source=feedblitz&utm_medium=FeedBlitzEmail&utm _content=812526&utm_campaign=0

Figure 4.1   Discretionary Funding for 2012: Defense

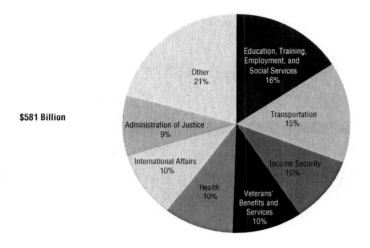

Source: Compiled by author with data from Elmendorf, Douglas W. and the Congressional Budget Office.
"Choices for Federal Spending and Taxes." September 17, 2012.
http://www.cbo.gov/publication/43619?utm_source=feedblitz&utm_medium=FeedBlitzEmail&utm
_content=812526&utm_campaign=0

Figure 4.2   Discretionary Funding for 2012: Non-defense

mandatory programs that spend whatever is needed to cover the costs of providing legislatively mandated benefits. The ease with which Congress can modify discretionary spending relative to mandatory spending has made it a convenient target for cuts in periods of concern over growing deficits.

As a catch all for most federal government activity, discretionary spending easily can be portrayed as the "big government" many decry, and trimming this or that portion of it seems relatively harmless. When forced to cut, targeting a few programs in the discretionary category poses fewer political risks than taking on major reform of the large, faster growing, and much more expensive entitlement programs. Although expansion of discretionary spending over the past decades and into the future has little to do with the problems of deficit and debt, it has borne the brunt of spending cuts over time. Many budget experts worry that the political barriers to restraining mandatory spending or raising taxes creates pressure for Congress to cut too far into core government responsibilities in the discretionary category. As pressure to reduce deficits and debt grows in the future, important public needs will go unmet as Washington politicians cut too deeply in the part of the budget labeled "discretionary."

Past and Future Trends in Discretionary Spending

Fifty years ago discretionary spending made up two-thirds of the total federal budget with mandatory and interest spending comprising only a third.[1] Today, the situation has been reversed with mandatory and interest spending now two-thirds of the budget and discretionary spending one third. This reversal has come about because of both the expansion of mandatory spending and the relative decline in defense spending. In 1962, defense spending made up fully one-half of total federal spending; it was under 20 percent of the budget in 2011. Viewed in terms of relative slices of the budget pies, federal entitlement spending to support the incomes and pay for the health care of, mostly elderly, Americans has replaced national defense as the country's chief priority.

Over this same period, non-defense discretionary spending has comprised a fairly constant 20 percent or so of the budget. In 1962, non-defense discretionary spending was 18.3 percent of the budget; expansion of social programs in the late 1960s raised the percentage to close to 25 for most of the 1970s; but Reagan administration cuts of those same programs slashed discretionary spending to about 16 percent of the total budget in the 1980s. Beginning in 2001, non-defense discretionary spending began to rise again and reached around 19 percent of the total budget. The overall spending trend of the past fifty years has been the shift from defense to entitlement spending.

Looking at discretionary spending as a percentage of GDP offers a more nuanced perspective of how this spending has changed in relation to the entire economy. In 1962, discretionary spending made up 12.7 percent of the entire economy with 9.3 percent of defense spending accounting for most of that figure. At that time, mandatory programs made up only 5.8 percent of GDP. By 2012, discretionary spending had dropped from 12.7 percent to only 8.3 percent of GDP with that entire decline coming from reduced defense spending as a percent of GDP. In 2012, non-defense discretionary spending, in fact, was slightly higher than it had been in 1962—4 percent of GDP instead of the 3.4 percent in 1962. This was still a decline, however, from the high point of non-defense discretionary spending in the 1970s when it made up 5 percent or more of GDP. Although non-defense spending as a percent of GDP has not dropped as much as defense spending, America still spends slightly more on defense, 4.3 percent of GDP, than it does on non-defense discretionary spending.

Future projections from both the Office of Management and Budget (OMB) and the Congressional Budget Office (CBO) show that, under current law, total discretionary spending will plummet in coming years. As early as 2017, it will drop 2 percent of GDP and continue to decline thereafter. By 2023, total discretionary spending will be between 5 and 6 percent of GDP with both defense and non-defense spending below 3 percent apiece.[2] If these declines come to pass, the federal government will have shrunk to levels of the 1950s relative to the size of the economy.

These projections raise serious questions about the capacity of the federal government to fulfill its core functions in coming decades. The services citizens have come to expect from federal agencies, from weather reports to air traffic control, would have to be curtailed. To see what is at stake, we need to dig a little more deeply into the details of what discretionary spending pays for.

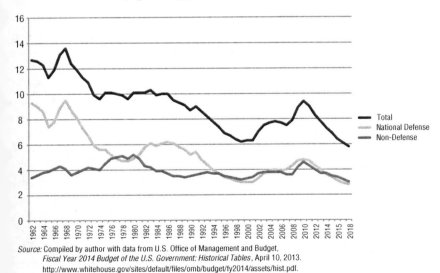

Source: Compiled by author with data from U.S. Office of Management and Budget, *Fiscal Year 2014 Budget of the U.S. Government: Historical Tables*, April 10, 2013. http://www.whitehouse.gov/sites/default/files/omb/budget/fy2014/assets/hist.pdf.

Figure 4.3 Discretionary Spending as a Percentage of GDP: 1962–2018

Non-Defense Discretionary Spending

This category of spending supports such a broad array of specific activities and touches the lives of Americans in so many diverse ways that drawing a clear picture of it and the implication of any future cuts is not a simple task. Because most of us take for granted many of the services that federal spending supports, describing what it means is doubly complex. When we look at the local weather report while we sip our morning coffee, how many of us think about the federal spending which funds the National Weather Service that provides the data and analysis for the local weather forecaster? This bit of federal spending not only helps us decide whether to take an umbrella to work, it also warns of pending natural disasters like hurricanes and tornadoes, keeps flying safer, and helps farmers know when to plant their crops.

We easily take for granted the wealth of information lots of government agencies provide for free that we constantly use in our daily lives. Few businesses could operate without the data on economic conditions and consumer behavior provided by the Census Bureau, Labor Department, U.S. Treasury, and the Commerce Department. Readers of this book (and its author) rely on the government agencies that produce and disseminate budget information. We may take much of what discretionary spending supports for granted, but when we consider it, few of us would consider what this spending produces is "discretionary." A brief look at three areas in the non-defense discretionary category will make this clear: basic scientific research, physical infrastructure, and public health.

Americans celebrate innovation and scientific discoveries. We chronicle the role of remarkable individuals, from Thomas Edison to Bill Gates, or innovative corporations, from AT&T to Apple, in transforming our lives. But the crucial role federally funded research in making much innovation possible is acknowledged hardly at all. Many of the scientific breakthroughs and inventions of the past one hundred years would not have come about without that portion of discretionary spending devoted to research. Federal funds provide about 80 percent of scientific research funding in the United States through agencies such as the National Science Foundation, the National Institutes of Health, and the Department of Energy.[3] Such basic research has been responsible for much of the technology we take for granted today from personal computers to medical diagnostic technology. According to the OMB, federal research and development funding is now half of what it was as a percentage of GDP in the 1960s. This drop in discretionary funding has had a serious impact on America's leadership in science and technology, with the United States losing its former dominance of scientific and engineering publications and new patents.

Discretionary funding also is a primary source of funds for the construction and maintenance of America's roads, bridges, dams, seaports, clean water systems, sewers, airports, and inland waterways. The federal government shares with state and local governments funding responsibility for national infrastructure, but federal support for these endeavors is crucial. The construction and maintenance of the Interstate Highway System, today the primary means for transporting people and goods across the nation, was one of the federal government's crowning achievements of the twentieth century—financed from discretionary spending.

For the past several decades, governments at all levels have failed to invest sufficiently in upgrading the nation's aging infrastructure. Public physical infrastructure investment, according to the OMB, varied between 4 and 5 percent of GDP in the 1950s and 60s, but has shrunk to under 2 percent in the last two decades. The American Society for Civil Engineers (ASCE) estimates that the nation will need to invest $3.6 trillion by the 2020s to support future economic growth.[4] This is the same period during which the CBO projects federal discretionary spending to drop by half. If this happens, the federal government will be unable to contribute its share of the infrastructure renewal that the ASCE says is needed.

Finally, for our last example of an area of non-defense discretionary spending, the federal government has major responsibility for assuring the health of the American public. The Centers for Disease Control has the lead responsibility for monitoring the nation's health, in particular watching for signs of new illnesses and their potential spread through the population. For example, it monitors the emergence of new strains of infectious disease, in particular new flu strains, around the world and implements plans for vaccine development and distribution to combat them. Federal agencies work in conjunction with state departments of health to promote vaccinations, monitor, and combat disease, and these state level departments depend greatly on federal grants, all from discretionary spending, to do their jobs.

In addition, the Food and Drug Administration and U.S. Department of Agriculture inspect the nation's food supply to assure it is fit for consumption, and they combat disease outbreaks from tainted food when these occur. Meat or vegetables tainted with salmonella or e coli bacteria get removed from store shelves thanks to discretionary spending. Moreover, this spending funds the National Institutes of Health and its research to find cures for diseases and develop new therapies and drugs.

Hundreds of other crucial federal programs fall into the non-defense discretionary spending category including national parks, space exploration, border control, education, public broadcasting, support for the arts and humanities. Few Americans would regard most of these as optional activities; they are needed to support a growing economy and the quality of life.

One would expect that a growing population and growing economy would require a corresponding increase in spending for these activities over time. The share of GDP, for example, devoted to these activities need not expand, although public leaders might opt to do so, but a decline in share could be dangerous for the nation's well-being. An expanding economy needs the support of additional investments in physical infrastructure, research and development, and education if it is to continue to grow. The level of spending on these things necessary to support our current $15 trillion economy will not be adequate for an economy that grows to $20 trillion, $25 trillion, $30 trillion and higher in the coming decades. This rising GDP also will support the living standards of a growing population which will require increased spending on public services. The number of federal judges, FBI agents, FDA inspectors, Customs agents, National Park Service staff, etc., will need to increase overtime to serve a larger population.

The percent of GDP devoted to non-defense discretionary spending, for the most part, provides a good gauge of whether public expenditure to support an growing economy and population remains adequate. If we are aware of what non-defense discretionary spending accomplishes, then projections of its decline relative to the size of the economy takes on a new meaning. The politics of deficits and debt becomes more than conflict over abstract spending categories; it is about the well-being of Americans and the quality of their lives in the twenty-first century.

Defense Discretionary Spending

Some critics express alarm at the implications of the decline of non-defense discretionary spending for the American standard of living, which echoes the worry some defense experts have in the decline of defense spending. In fact, the defense decline relative to GDP has been more dramatic. As Figure 4.3 shows, over the past fifty years defense spending as a percentage of GDP has declined from about 9 percent to a little over 3 percent. Advocates for national defense spending often point to this decline as evidence that military spending should be off limits as a means of deficit reduction. This argument assumes that defense spending relative to GDP provides an appropriate measure of the adequacy of such spending. Unlike non-defense discretionary spending which, as argued above, needs to grow as our economy and population expand, defense spending can decline relative to GDP without undermining the needs it seeks to meet.

Defense spending is needed to protect against threats to national security. Its adequacy depends on the nature of those threats and how much spending is needed to meet them. How much of our national resources must be devoted to protecting the country from foreign enemies will vary over time depending on the severity of the threats and the cost of meeting them. In 1962, at the height of the Cold War, for example, a much higher proportion of GDP devoted to national defense, given the size of the overall economy at the time, was required to deter the military might of the Soviet Union. By contrast, the decline in defense spending relative to GDP two decades later (see Figure 4.3) was mainly a consequence of a growing economy rather than any large reduction in spending on national security. During the mid-1970s, after the end of the Vietnam War, defense spending in real, inflation controlled dollars was only slightly less than it had been in the early 1960s ($390 billion in 1962 compared to $312 billion in 1977).[5] This spending level as a percent of GDP was now half of what it had been in the early 60s, not because actual defense spending was half as large but because the GDP was so much larger.

The rise in spending relative to GDP during the 1980s was a result of the Reagan defense spending increases in respond to perceptions of Soviet military aggression and this dropped off after the end of the Cold War in 1989. The precipitous fall of defense spending relative to the economy between 1984 and the late 1990s was not exclusively a function of the end of the Cold War, however. Rapid economic growth in the 1990s pushed up the GDP making the decline in defense spending appear greater than it actually was in real terms. Defense spending as a percent of the economy declined by half between the mid-1980s, but in terms of real dollars was cut back by only 25 percent as the Cold War wound down. As a matter of arithmetic, if defense spending were to remain a constant percentage of GDP, then, as the economy grew, real defense spending would have to grow, irrespective of the actual foreign threats facing the nation. A more fiscally responsible way to budget for defense is to spend what is needed to meet foreign threats at a given time.

Specific foreign conflicts also require devoting increased national resources to defense spending, usually producing a rise in such spending relative to GDP. For example, the spike in defense spending as a percentage of GDP after 1966 reflected increased spending for the Vietnam War. The winding down of this spending contributed to the rapid decline after 1969. Increased defense spending relative to GDP after the events of 9/11/2001 also can be attributed both to new terror threats and to the conflicts in Iraq and Afghanistan (see Figure 4.3). The spike in 2008 also is partly a consequence of a shrunken GDP during the Great Recession. To sum up, evaluating spending in relation to GDP always needs to consider both changes in actual spending and changes in economic growth.

In evaluating the adequacy of defense discretionary spending, then, it makes more sense to look at actual levels of spending in real dollars and in light of potential security threats. When we look at these data, it is hard to make the case that current level of defense spending is too low. In 2010, the United States spent $610 billion in inflation controlled dollars on national defense.[6] This amount was higher than at any year since the end of WWII. When the Cold War was at its height and the Vietnam War raging in 1968, defense spending was $519 billion; at the peak of the Reagan build up in 1989, defense cost $482 billion. Some argue that current high levels of defense expenditure are a result of the need to combat terrorism around the globe and fight wars in Iraq and Afghanistan. (The latter were a factor in the 2010 high; diminished spending on these wars brought defense spending down to $574 billion by 2012.)

But critics of these high levels of defense spending question whether current national security threats demand more spending than was needed during the Cold War to counter a potent super power enemy. In today's world, there is no potential adversary comparable to what the Soviet Union was in the 1960s or even the 1980s. In 2012, the United States spent more on defense than the next ten largest militaries in the world combined.[7] Also, eight of those on this latter list are currently staunch U.S. allies, such as Great Britain, France, and Germany, and only two, Russia and China, might be seen as future potential adversaries. Of the latter two, China poses the greater long-term security threat, but in 2012, it spent only one-quarter of what the United States spends. Currently, the United States has ten aircraft carriers deployed around the world.[8] That is equal to all the aircraft carriers in service in navies of all other world powers, and of these, only one deploys more than one carrier—Italy, which has two. At present, the United States has overwhelming military power in comparison to any other nations and spends much more. Even if one takes into account our nation's concerns for combating terrorism around the world or the need for readiness to engage in conflicts in smaller nations, like Iraq, current and projected levels of military expenditure seem ample to keep the nation secure.

The United States may have to worry about the size of its military in the future as China's military grows or some new threat develops. Future threats might require more defense discretionary spending. In addition, the cost of new military technology and coping with new kinds of threats such as cyber war will require continued spending needs. Technological innovation and military research and development do track economic growth in ways comparable to non-defense discretionary spending, supporting a case for keeping this proportion of defense spending rising with economic growth. But, overall, a case can be made that reductions in military spending may be able to play a role in reducing future deficits.

Discretionary Spending and Future Debt

Controlling discretionary spending ought to be only a small part of the politics of deficit and debt. In comparison with mandatory spending, both categories of discretionary spending have contributed little to the rise in government spending in the past couple of decades and are not a major factor in future deficits. Of course, prudent fiscal policy does require restraint in discretionary spending just like all spending, if future debt is to be controlled. Defense discretionary spending, especially, may be an area where savings can be found. However, the greatest fiscal policy challenge will be making sure that needed discretionary spending not be cut too much.

Up until now, as Part II of this book will make clear, the politics of deficit and debt has put too much emphasis on discretionary spending. The political obstacles to reducing mandatory spending or raising taxes have led Congress to slash discretionary spending in ways that will likely harm the American economy in the long run and even make our debt problem worse. Sufficient public investment in U.S. society, which means discretionary spending, is as important to the standard of living of future generations as keeping future debt under control. The dysfunctional politics of deficit and debt, however, may put these needed investments at risk in the name of securing future Americans from the burden of debt.

Notes

1. Budget figures in the following paragraphs are taken from Office and Management and Budget, *Fiscal Year 2014 – Historical Tables* (Washington, D.C.: U.S. Government Printing Office, 2013).
2. Niraj Chokshi, "The Budget Debate in 6 Simple Graphics," *The National Journal*, May 8, 2013 (http://www.nationaljournal.com/congress/the-budget-debate-in-6-simple-graphics-20130508).
3. Task Force on American Innovation *American Exceptionalism, American Decline?: Research, the Knowledge Ecnomy, and the 21st Century Challenge* pp. 9–10 (http://www.innovationtaskforce.org/docs/Benchmarks%20-%20 2012.pdf).
4. American Society for Civil Engineers, *2013 Report Card for America's Infrastructure* (http://www.infrastructurereportcard.org/).
5. These figures are FY 2005 dollars and taken from Office and Management and Budget, *Fiscal Year 2014 – Historical Tables*, Table 8.8.
6. Ibid.
7. Stockholm International Peace Research Institute, "Recent Trends in Military Expenditure" April 2013 (http://www.sipri.org/research/armaments/milex/recent-trends).
8. Walter Hickey and Robert Johnson, "These are the 20 Aircraft Carriers in Service today" The Business Insider (http://www.businessinsider.com/the-20-in-service-aircraft-carriers-patrolling-the-world-today-2012-8?op=1).

5

RAISING FEDERAL TAX REVENUE

Public opinion polls consistently show that Americans regard their tax burden as too high. A recent Gallup poll found only about one-third of respondents satisfied with their level of taxation.[1] For most of the last three decades, clear majorities, sometimes rising to nearly 70 percent, say they pay too much federal tax. These perceptions are all the more remarkable since, as we shall see, tax rates have trended downward during these decades and the average tax burden on Americans also has decreased. The taxes Americans pay are some of the lowest among industrial democracies. Yet, in spite of these realities, many Americans consider their burden of taxation unfair. These views pose a difficult challenge when it comes to addressing deficits and debt. While we Americans want government to provide an extensive range of services and benefits, we resist raising the revenue to pay for them. If we want to reduce future deficits without a drastic change in what we want from government, tax revenues will need to rise. This chapter provides some perspective on the federal tax system, its evolution, and issues connected with looking to tax revenue to reduce deficit and debt.

A Brief History of the U.S. Tax System

Until World War II, federal taxation directly affected only a very small percentage of Americans.[2] Throughout the nineteenth century, except for a few years during the Civil War, a small federal government relied almost exclusively on tariffs and excise taxes to finance its operations. Raising more government revenue through a tax on incomes to support a more activist government was a central goal of the Progressive movement in the early twentieth century. In 1913, this goal was realized in the ratification of the Sixteenth Amendment to the Constitution which authorized Congress to enact a tax on incomes. In short order, Congress imposed a tax on individual incomes and on corporate income.

For the next three decades the federal income tax generated more revenue for the federal government, but only from a thin slice of the wealthiest Americans—most Americans earned incomes well below the personal exemption. In 1940, only 3 percent of income earners were subject to federal income tax. The need for more revenue to finance World War II changed that, and, by 1945, about 30 percent of Americans were paying income tax. Post-war prosperity and rising incomes brought steadily increasing numbers of Americans into the income tax system. In addition to the income tax, by the 1950s nearly all Americans also paid payroll taxes, first imposed in 1936, to support the Social Security system. The income tax, the payroll tax (FICA), and a separate income tax on corporations have been the principal sources of federal revenue for the past seventy years.

The federal income tax system that emerged in the first decades after World War II included around twenty-five tax "brackets"—income ranges taxed at different rates including a very high top marginal tax rate. In 1945, the top marginal tax rate was 94 percent on all income over $200,000 (about $2.4 million in today's dollars). Keep in mind that this rate applied only to the income over the top bracket amount so that, even for the fraction of taxpayers subject to the top rate, it applied only to a part of their total income. Most of their income was taxed at the much lower rates applied to the lower brackets. Also, many wealthy taxpayers could take advantage of many tax deductions, exclusions, and credits that lowered their taxable income below the top marginal rate. The major change in the federal income system since that time has been a series of reductions of both the number of tax brackets and the marginal tax rates, in comparison, the marginal rates of the immediate post-war period now seem unimaginably high.

The first major rate reductions occurred in the early 1960s when the Kennedy administration sought to stimulate economic demand in Keynesian fashion with a major tax cut. This cut reduced the top marginal rate to 70 percent and spurred that decade's rapid economic growth. Although this cut was adopted using a Keynesian rationale, later advocates of *supply-side* tax cuts would point to the Kennedy rate cuts and the rapid economic growth that followed to support their case for hefty tax rate cuts when Ronald Reagan won the presidency in 1980. Reagan would embrace the new supply-side philosophy as the formula for solving the economic troubles he faced upon assuming office.

Slower economic growth plus three recessions during the 1970s had produced record unemployment *combined with* unprecedented high inflation. Traditional Keynesian demand management, which called for higher government spending to combat unemployment but spending reduction to combat inflation, had no answers when inflation and unemployment occurred simultaneously. Reagan's advisors offered an alternative to Keynesian demand management with a supply-side analysis that argued that stagnant growth resulted from high marginal tax rates. They claimed that the *supply* of investment and work in the economy was too low because government taxed away too much of the additional income earned from new investment and work. According to this argument, everyone held back the supply of productive resources for fear that too much of the additional income earned from investing resources or working longer hours would be taxed away. The solution was to change the economic incentives in the tax code through an across the board reduction in marginal tax rates. In addition, the supply-siders argued, the surge of economic productivity that these tax cuts would produce would be so great that the tax cuts would eventually produce more revenue for government rather than less. Large tax cuts to spur growth could be had without increasing government deficits.

In 1981, Congress passed Reagan's supply-side tax cut, dramatically cutting tax rates and reducing the number of brackets. The top marginal rate dropped immediately from 70 percent to 50 percent with further gradual reductions during the decade down to 28 percent. Comparable reductions occurred in lower tax brackets, and the number of brackets was reduced eventually to five. In the wake of these tax reductions, income tax revenue declined significantly, but economic growth also picked up. (Many economists later would argue that the Reagan tax cuts promoted growth because of their effect on economic demand rather than supply-side effects.) The supposed supply-side increase in tax revenue did not materialize and, as Reagan greatly increased military spending and did not significantly cut spending elsewhere, deficits ballooned to the highest levels in the post-WWII period. These high *structural* deficits persisted all during the economic expansion of the decade.

Both of Reagan's successors, George H.W. Bush and Bill Clinton, alarmed by the high structural deficits, raised taxes, bringing the top marginal rate up to 39 percent by 1993. The Clinton tax increase combined with spending restraint and strong economic growth produced economic surpluses at the end of the decade. These surpluses, however, gave George W. Bush an excuse for another round of tax cuts. Arguing that the surplus should be "returned to the taxpayer" and also mustering again supply-side arguments, Bush cut back the top marginal rate to 35 percent. The Bush tax cuts included a gradual phasing out of the estate tax plus maintained lower taxes on capital gains (profits made on sale of stocks and bonds) and dividends (corporate profits distributed to stockholders) as enacted under Clinton. In order to keep the projected cost of the tax cuts low, the Bush tax cut law had the unusual feature providing for an end to the tax cuts (and a return to the Clinton rates) after ten years. Before that time, Bush and his Republican allies assumed Congress could be convinced to make the tax cuts permanent. In 2003, a second round of Bush tax cuts lowered taxes on capital gains and dividends to 15 percent, the lowest level since the 1930s. Like the Reagan tax cuts, the Bush cuts increased the structural deficits, but, unlike the Reagan cuts, failed to stimulate an economic

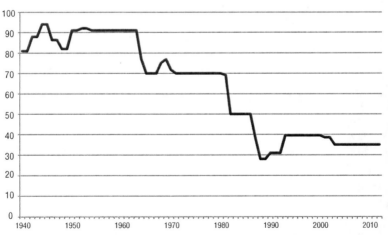

Source: Compiled by author with data from Tax Policy Center. "U.S. Individual Income Tax: Personal Exemptions and Lowest and Highest Tax Bracket Tax Rates and Tax Base for Regular Tax, Tax Years 1913-2013." April 10, 2013. http://www.taxpolicycenter.org/taxfacts/displayafact.cfm?Docid=543

Figure 5.1 Highest Marginal Income Tax Rates, 1940–2012

boom as economic growth remained slow throughout his term, ending in the Great Recession of 2008.

Finally, during most of this period of tax rate reductions, the tax code included a peculiar feature that affected only a small percentage of taxpayers, but would become a significant factor in debates over the future of deficits and debt—*the Alternative Minimum Tax* (AMT). First enacted in 1969, the AMT was intended to assure that the wealthy could not use exotic tax avoidance strategies and tax shelters to elude paying any income taxes. Wealthier taxpayers earning income above a certain exemption amount were required to calculate their taxes both under ordinary tax rates, with allowances for regular deductions and exemptions, and under a separate AMT procedure that did not allow for most tax breaks. If the tax using the AMT procedure was higher, the taxpayer paid that amount.

The AMT law, however, did not provide for linking the exemption amount to inflation. Consequently, over time, this tax provision aimed at the wealthiest taxpayers had the potential to include ordinary middle-class individuals. To prevent this from happening, Congress has periodically raised the exemption amount, but it has never indexed the AMT to inflation. If the exemption were not raised, the AMT would steadily cover an ever-increasing proportion of taxpayers. Yet, eliminating the AMT or indexing it permanently to inflation would deny the federal government a significant amount of future revenues. The Tax Policy Center estimates that an AMT inflation-linked exemption would reduce federal revenues between 2013 and 2022 by $2.7 trillion dollars.[3]

The Tax Burden: Who Does and Does Not Pay Taxes?

While the trend for the past fifty years has been for individual income tax rates to decline, the opposite has been true for payroll taxes. Beginning in the 1950s, Congress periodically increased the payroll tax rate for Social Security and the amount of income subject to tax to cover the increasing costs of the program. The creation of Medicare in 1965 added a small additional tax to fund that program. The Greenspan reforms in 1983 raised the payroll tax rate substantially and, at the same time, put in place automatic gradual increases in the amount of salary subject to tax. The combined result produced an increase in the average payroll tax rate for individual workers from 6.8 percent of household income in 1979 to 8.0 percent in 2009.[4] Over this same period, Americans saw their average income tax rates fall from a peak of 11.9 percent of household income prior to the Reagan tax cuts to a historic low of 7.2 percent in 2009. Taken together, however, the overall average burden of federal taxes has fallen significantly since 1979, declining from 22.0 percent of income in 1979 to only 17.4 percent in 2009 (see Figure 5.2). Part of the recent drop in tax burden resulted in loss of income from the 2008 recession, but, prior to the recession in 2007, average effective tax rates had dropped to 20 percent. Even though many Americans may perceive an overall increase in their tax burden, the statistics show that federal taxes take less, on average, from household incomes than they did thirty years ago.

This decrease in tax burden has occurred across all income categories, although they have been most dramatic for the very wealthy and the poor. The top 1 percent of income earners paid on average about 37 percent of their income in taxes in 1979 but less than 30 percent in 2007, prior to income losses incurred in the recession (see Figure 5.3). According to the Congressional Budget Office (CBO), much of the drop in the tax burden of the top 1 percent can be attributed to the Bush era tax policies.[5] Because wealthier taxpayers earn a larger

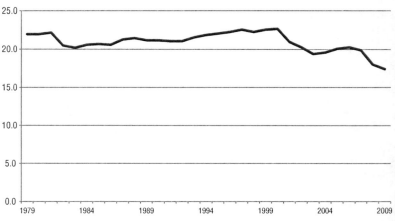

Source: Compiled by author with data from Tax Policy Center. "Average Federal Tax Rates for All Households, by Comprehensive Household Income Quintile, 1979-2009." October 24, 2012.
http://www.taxpolicycenter.org/taxfacts/displayafact.cfm?Docid=456

Figure 5.2   Average Federal Tax Rate, 1979–2009

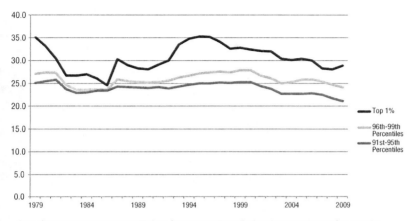

Source: Compiled by author with data from Tax Policy Center. "Average Federal Tax Rates for All Households, by Comprehensive Household Income Quintile, 1979 -2009." October 24, 2012. http://www.taxpolicycenter.org/taxfacts/displayafact.cfm?Docid=456

Figure 5.3   Tax Rates for the Top 10% of Taxpayers, 1979–2009

share of total income, cuts in tax rates benefit them more, in terms of the total dollars gained, than lower income tax payers. For example, between 2004 and 2012, taxpayers earning $1 million or more in income averaged a tax cut of over $1 million while someone earning between $50 and $75,000 received a $13,000 tax cut.[6] Lower taxes on capital gains and dividends also benefitted wealthy taxpayers disproportionately because a high proportion of their total income comes from those sources rather than salaries and wages.

The poor also saw a decrease in tax burden because of a combination of declining wages at the lower end of the wage spectrum and the effects of more generous EITC benefits beginning in the 1990s (see Figure 5.4). The trend toward lower tax rates since the 1980s that benefitted the rich coincided with the enactment of more generous tax credits, that is, direct reductions in tax liability for the very poor. The most important was a substantial increase over this period in the Earned Income Tax Credit. First enacted in the 1970s, the EITC has had strong support from both conservatives and liberals. In fact, the idea originated among conservative thinkers, like economist Milton Friedman, who saw supplementing the income of the working poor with tax credits as a superior way to help the poor than cash welfare payments. Unlike welfare, EITC goes only to those who earn some income and thus provides

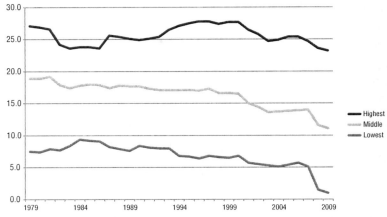

Source: Compiled by author with data from Tax Policy Center. "Average Federal Tax Rates for All Households, by Comprehensive Household Income Quintile, 1979-2009." October 24, 2012. http://www.taxpolicycenter.org/taxfacts/displayafact.cfm?Docid=456

Figure 5.4 Tax Rates for Highest, Middle, and Lowest Income Quintiles, 1979–2009

an incentive to work, even at the low wage jobs that may be the only alternative available for the very poor with few skills.

Congresses in both the Reagan and Clinton years expanded the credit with large bipartisan majorities. In addition, bipartisan majorities adopted a Clinton administration recommendation in 1997 to create the Child Tax Credit which, although available to families earning up to $110,000, had a substantial impact on the incomes of the poor. Both types of credits are refundable, that is, they are paid to the taxpayer even if the credit exceeds the amount of tax owed. So, in effect, for low income tax payers who owe little tax, they serve as direct income subsidies. These two tax credits combined have become the principal means for lifting the poor, particularly poor children, out of poverty.[7]

As a result of these credits, the bottom 20 percent of income earners had their federal tax burden cut in half from 8 percent of income to around 4 percent. (The dramatic loss of income for this group in the 2008 recession has driven its average federal tax rate down to about 1 percent.) The middle of the income distribution (quintiles 2–4) fared not quite as well, but still saw a substantial decrease from about 19 percent of income in 1979 to 15 percent in 2007. The overall story, then, is of a federal income tax system that taxes substantially less of the income from Americans today than prior to the Reagan era of tax reduction in the 1980s.

Although wealthy Americans experienced a drop in their federal tax bill over the past three decades, the federal tax system overall remains progressive—the higher one's income, the higher percentage of tax one pays. The average effective tax rate for the 1 percent of earners in 2008 was 31.6 percent. As the average rate declines in step wise fashion as income declines, the lowest 20 percent paid on average of only 1.1 percent of their income in federal taxes (see Figure 5.4).

Progressive taxation usually is justified for several reasons. First, wealthier people have a greater ability to pay because their higher incomes give them more discretionary income that is not needed for necessities. Economists often make this point in terms of the "law of diminishing returns." This concept argues that the value to an individual of any good diminishes with each additional unit one consumes. Anyone who attempts to eat three ice cream cones in a row understands this concept. As it is with ice cream, the economist argues, so too with money. The more money I have, the less I value the last dollar earned. So taking a higher percentage of a richer person's income involves taking dollars that person values less than someone who possesses fewer dollars. Second, the more income one has, the more one benefits from the order and stability that government provides. All, of course, benefit from government services, but they are worth more to those with more income and wealth to protect. Or considered from a slightly different perspective, if living in a stable productive society has allowed me to prosper, I have a greater responsibility to support the government that makes that possible than someone who has prospered less.

Finally, progressive taxation reduces somewhat the income inequalities that the economic marketplace naturally creates. Taxing richer taxpayers at higher rates than those with less income makes the post-tax income distribution more equal than the pre-tax distribution. Greater income equality, according to advocates of progressive taxation, reduces social division, potential unrest, and increases social solidarity. Although the current federal tax system is progressive, it has become less so during the past three decades.[8] The reductions in top marginal tax rates, lower corporate tax rates, lower estate taxes, and lower rates on capital gains combined with greater reliance on the regressive payroll tax reduced the tax burden of wealthier Americans relative to those with lower incomes. (A regressive tax is the opposite of a progressive one—it taxes those with lower incomes at higher rates than higher income earners.)

Federal taxes continue to be progressive, despite tax rate cuts that benefit the wealthy and increases in regressive payroll taxes, because a substantial proportion of the population does not pay income taxes.[9] Many people earn such low incomes that the personal and dependent exemptions and the standard deduction add up to more than their total income so they owe no tax. The EITC and Child Tax Credit further increase the number of taxpayers without tax liability. The percentage of Americans who owed no income tax grew substantially as a result of the 2008 recession. In 2009, for example, 51 percent of households paid no income tax, but this was a temporary situation, and, as the economy recovered, the percentage paying no income tax dropped to 46 percent in 2011. Future economic growth will mean a rising percentage of households will pay income tax, with the percentage not paying tax dropping to the pre-recession average of around 40 percent of households.

Even though some workers do not pay income taxes, this does not mean that they pay no federal tax. Nearly all workers pay the FICA and Medicare payroll taxes and, since these are regressive taxes, they take a larger proportion of low income workers' incomes than those earning more. Only about one-third of those who do not pay income tax also pay no payroll tax, and these are primarily elderly and disabled people unable to work. If one adds state and local taxes, which also tend to be regressive, the overall tax burden on low income households rises substantially. Taking into account state sales taxes and property taxes along with federal payroll taxes, the lowest fifth of income earners paid over 17 percent of their income in taxes in 2011.[10] In sum, everyone in America pays some tax. While the overall federal system is progressive, lower income households still bear a substantial tax burden when the tax system as a whole is taken into account.

The Tax Burden: Historical and International Comparisons

Some Americans concerned with "big government" seem to believe that the overall federal tax burden in relation to the economy has grown over time. In reality, as we have seen, federal tax revenue as a proportion of GDP has remained quite stable at around 18 percent since the 1970s. The size tends to fluctuate around that percentage in response to tax rate cuts, which tend to drive it lower, and economic growth and inflation, both of which send it higher. As individuals' incomes rise, whether through higher incomes or inflation, they move into higher tax brackets and pay higher taxes as a result. During the 1970s, high inflation rates pushed federal revenues as a percent of GDP to nearly 20 percent. The Reagan tax cuts combined with lower inflation brought the level down to around 17 percent by the end of the decade. Higher rates combined with robust growth raised federal revenues again to 20 percent of GDP by 2000, but the sizable Bush tax cuts lowered the percentage to 16 percent after 2003. The massive economic downturn in 2008 combined with the lower Bush tax rates brought federal revenues to 15 percent of GDP, the lowest level since the 1950s. This rapid decline in revenues contributed greatly to the large deficits starting in 2009. The CBO projects that federal tax revenue as a percent of GDP ought to return to around 18 percent once the economy recovers.

Compared to other democracies, taxes in the United States are quite low, even when state and local taxes are included. In 2007, total taxes as a percent of GDP in the United States were just under 30 percent of GDP, which is lower than most European democracies plus Canada, New Zealand, and South Korea.[11] Two European counties, Denmark and Sweden, have tax levels equal to half their entire GDP while most other European democracies range from 37 percent in Germany to 42 percent in Belgium. Even our Canadian neighbors to the north pay taxes equal to 35 percent of their economy. Most of these other rich democracies have higher tax levels and also provide more generous social benefits to their citizens. In comparison to these countries, government in the United States seems not "big" but "small."

Tax Expenditures

Up to now I have described how the amount of revenue the federal government collects depends on a combination of tax rates, the proportion of income or wages taxed, and the performance of the economy. There remains another important factor greatly affecting the amount of revenue collected—how the tax laws define income subject to taxation. Sometimes called tax "loopholes," a variety of exclusions, deductions, exemptions, and credits substantially reduce the amount of tax revenue collected. Examples include: the federal government promotes private health insurance coverage by excluding from taxable income the premium benefits employers pay for their employees' health insurance. Home ownership is encouraged by allowing taxpayers to deduct from their taxable income the interest paid on a home mortgage. The child tax credit, discussed earlier, allows taxpayers to reduce their tax bill by a certain amount for each of their children. Businesses receive a variety of deductions and credits for particular kinds of investments. In addition to these measures that reduce income subject to tax, the tax code also provides preferential lower rates on certain types of income, such as the lower rate on capital gains and dividends. The deduction for charitable giving encourages philanthropy and provides financial support to a wide variety of non-profit causes from churches to symphony orchestras.

Congress has passed these various loopholes to encourage certain activities like home ownership, purchase of health insurance, or raising children, because it considers them valuable to American society. Some are aimed at individual taxpayers, as in these examples, but others are aimed at certain business activities. In both cases, Congress uses the tax code to commit public resources, potential tax revenue, to these activities. The label tax *expenditure* is appropriate because these tax preferences subsidize the particular activity. The effect would be the same if Congress collected the tax and then voted to spend government funds to support the activity. For example, instead of providing parents with a tax credit for each child, the federal government could provide the same subsidy through a benefit payment, as many European countries do. Tax expenditures are less visible than spending in the budget and have provided a popular way for members of Congress to subsidize valued causes without appearing to increase government spending.

Tax expenditures taken together are often called America's "hidden welfare state" because they provide social benefits, such as support for home ownership and child support, through the tax code rather than through federal spending.[12] Tax expenditures also are a form of mandatory spending because, like Social Security and Medicare, their cost is not subject to the annual budget process. The amount of revenue that goes uncollected each year because of the home mortgage deduction depends on the number of homeowners with mortgages and the size of their interest payments. Tax expenditures also are entitlements, just like the entitlement to Medicare or Food Stamps, so those who qualify are entitled to receive the benefits by law.

All told, tax expenditures cost the federal government a trillion dollars in 2012, equivalent to nearly the entire deficit for that year. They obviously have a tremendous impact on the overall federal budget. The CBO estimates that between 2012 and 2022, tax expenditures will total over 12 trillion dollars, an amount greater than the cost of Social Security or defense over the same period.[13] While some of the tax expenditures, like the EITC and Child Tax Credit described above, help poor families, most of the cost of tax expenditures derives from the large popular ones, like the income exemption for health insurance payments and the home mortgage insurance deduction, which primarily benefit middle-class and wealthy taxpayers. The overall impact of tax expenditures is regressive because as income grows, one derives greater benefit from them.

How Tax Rates Affect Revenue and Economic Growth

Since Ronald Reagan's presidency, the supply-side revolution that has fueled the declining tax rates of the past three decades has offered two fundamental promises. First, supply-side advocates claimed that reducing tax rates would spur rapid economic growth. Second, they claimed that the economic growth brought about by lower rates would be so strong as to eventually increase federal tax revenue. These two promises combined led to the counter-intuitive conclusion that federal taxes could be cut without increasing deficits and debt—no matter what happened with federal spending. Supply-siders seemed to portray cutting taxes as a magical elixir that would both revive the economy and relieve debt worries. Tax cuts were the proverbial "free lunch." Unfortunately, like all magical promises of free lunches, reality did not deliver.

Standard economic theory does support the idea that cutting tax rates can spur economic activity. In particular, lowering *marginal* tax rates, the percent of tax one pays on the last dollar earned, means a taxpayer gets to keep a higher percentage of income earned from additional work or investment. If I know I will get to keep 75 percent of the money I earn from a second job rather than only 60 percent, the logic argues, I will be more apt to take that second job. The same logic applies to investing in a new business or business expansion. If lower rates have this effect on individuals all across the economy, then one should expect an overall increase in economic activity and economic growth. The economic logic here seems airtight. All things being equal, if the government taxes less of new economic activity, then there ought to be more economic activity. Unfortunately for tidy economic theories, all things are never equal when it comes to the complex incentives that influence economic behavior. Three simple thought experiments illustrate this complexity.

First, a tax cut's impact on additional work and investment on individual behavior depends on the mix of incentives affecting economic activity. If I need a second job to feed my family, I am going to take the job whether I keep 75 percent or 60 percent of my wages. Similarly, if I have reason to believe that a lot of people will buy an innovative new product, I am likely to invest in making it whether my tax rate is 25 percent or 40 percent. No matter what the tax rate, I will make a lot of money selling lots of what I have to sell. And, if demand for my product is low, then no matter how low the tax rate, I am not going to invest in producing what I cannot sell.

Second, even if one accepts that tax rates affect incentives to work and invest, the impact they have on behavior will depend on the magnitude of changes. While I might turn down a second job if 50 percent of my wages were taxed away, a 10 percent reduction of tax rates, say from 30 to 20 percent, might not matter too much to me. I will take the job at either rate. Supply-siders argue that just as reducing tax rates increasing economic activity, raising taxes will accomplish the reverse—lower economic activity. Yet the impact on tax rates likely will depend on their magnitude in the context of the other factors that affect decisions to work or invest.

Finally, the claim that tax reductions always lead to more investment and work assumes that everyone has an insatiable desire for additional income. While this is a reasonable assumption under conditions of extreme scarcity, in more affluent societies individuals have more freedom to choose how much effort they wish to take to earn additional income. If there is an upper limit to the income I think I need for a satisfactory life, then a tax cut might cause me to reduce my economic activity rather than increase it. For example, if my income goal is to earn $100,000 and I make $90,000 now after taxes, a tax cut that raises my after tax income to $110,000 may lead me to *cut back* my work effort rather than increase it.

These three thought experiments show that like all types of behavior, economic behavior is complex: the impact of tax rates on this behavior will depend on the context and range of choices individuals have. In addition to the varied individual responses to changing tax incentives, a variety of factors besides tax rates influence economic growth. Access to raw materials, the levels of skills of workers, technological improvements, and the overall level of economic demand are just some of the many factors that, along with taxes, influence levels of economic activity. While no one would deny that tax rates deserve a place among relevant factors, empirical evidence suggests that levels of taxation may not be all that significant for economic growth.

The U.S. experience with tax cuts and tax increases over the past thirty years provides little support with the supply-side view that marginal tax rates have a major impact on economic activity. The Reagan tax cuts, taking effect during a recession, did contribute to spurring economic growth in the early 1980s, but they did so by helping to stimulate economic demand rather than promoting increased work and investment. In fact, economic studies of the period found no evidence that the Reagan tax cuts stimulated either increased work effort or increased savings and investment.[14] When the Clinton administration raised taxes in 1993, supply-side critics predicted dire economic effects, but the higher tax rates did not impede the economic boom of the decade. They did, however, contribute to increasing revenue flowing to the federal government and helped bring about the surpluses by the decade's end. Nor did the Bush tax cuts of 2001 or 2003 bring about strong economic growth; in fact, economic growth was feeble in the wake of these cuts.

In sum, the evidence from recent years suggests that, although tax rates may have some impact on economic activity, the magnitude of tax changes over the last thirty years has not been sufficient to have a major effect on levels of growth.[15] A comprehensive analysis by the Congressional Research Service of the impact of changes in tax rates since 1945 concluded that such changes "do not appear correlated with economic growth."[16] Even though tax cuts can contribute to a short-term Keynesian stimulus during a recession, during periods of economic expansion, as in the 1990s, sustained growth seems compatible with a wide range of tax rates.

International comparisons support this proposition. If supply-side theories were correct, one would expect that those countries with the lowest tax levels would be the most prosperous. When one compares tax levels with relative levels of prosperity among generally affluent countries, however, there is no correlation. In 2000, among prosperous countries with average GDP per person ranging from about $25–$30,000, tax levels varied from a low of 27 percent of GDP in Japan to nearly 55 percent in Sweden with most scattered in between.[17] The United States did have a higher GDP per person ($35,000) than most of these countries and also a tax level of 30 percent of GDP (including federal, state, and local taxes) that was lower than most. But Norway and little Luxembourg managed higher GDPs per capita than the United States with much higher tax levels of over 40 percent of GDP. Different levels of prosperity between countries must be related to other factors besides overall levels of taxation.

If supply-side tax cuts did not have the impact on rates of economic growth that advocates claimed, then they certainly could not fulfill the second promise—that they would not increase federal deficits. In fact, the experience with both the Reagan and Bush tax cuts was that they did significantly reduce federal revenues and add to the structural deficit. Deficits rose to the highest levels in the post-war period after the Reagan tax cuts and rose as well in the wake of the Bush cuts. Looking at how the level of federal revenues as a percent of GDP changed after the tax cuts provides the best measure of their impact. The Reagan cuts reduced federal revenue as a percent of GDP from 19.6 percent in 1981 to 18.4 percent in 1989, and after the Bush cuts, federal revenues as a percent of GDP fell from slightly over 20 percent in 2000 to just over 18 percent in 2007 prior to the recession.[18] As we saw earlier, the low Bush tax rates were a major factor contributing to the astronomical deficits during the 2008 recession when revenues as a percent of GDP fell to a sixty year low of 15 percent. The experience of the past thirty years confirms the common sense view that lowering tax rates results in less government revenue. The supply-side free lunch fantasy that taxes can be cut without affecting government deficits has proved, alas, a fantasy.

Conclusion

Although many Americans believe that federal taxes are too high, the evidence shows that the reality of the tax burden does not support this belief. Beginning with the Reagan supply-side tax cuts, income tax rates have taken a downward trajectory for the past thirty years, and this lighter income tax burden has largely offset higher payroll taxes for Social Security and Medicare. Americans, on average, pay a slightly lower effective tax rate than they did in 1979. The wealthy, thanks to much lower top marginal tax rates and lower taxes on investment income, and the poor, thanks to more generous tax credits, have benefitted most from lighter federal taxation. Even with these changes, the U.S. federal tax system remains progressive although slightly less so than in the 1960s. And, despite a slightly lower tax burden, the system has generated a constant level of revenue, around 18 percent of GDP, for the entire period. This revenue level, however, has not been sufficient, except for a few years in the late 1990s, to pay for federal spending commitments. The result has been relatively high structural deficits going back to the 1980s. Clearly, too little federal tax revenue is a component of our deficit and debt problem.

The 2008 recession produced huge deficits partly because of the interaction of low tax rates enacted during the Bush administration and the drop in household income. The historically low level of federal revenue as percent of GDP (15 percent) is an artifact of the recession and will rise as the economy recovers. Even if tax revenues return to their average level of the past few decades, will that be enough to fund future spending commitments? The answer most certainly is no. The tax system that has failed to generate sufficient revenue to avoid structural deficits for most of the past three decades clearly will be inadequate to meet the growing spending promised in existing laws. Entitlement reform may revise those promises somewhat and lower the upward spending trajectory, but the reality of an aging population suggests that higher future federal spending levels are inevitable. If an explosion of national debt is to be avoided, more federal tax revenue will have to be raised. Whether that comes from merely higher rates in the current system or more comprehensive tax reform will be the real choice facing policy makers.

Notes

1. A summary of Gallup polls regarding American's attitudes toward taxes can be found at http://www.gallup.com/poll/1714/Taxes.aspx#1.
2. Two good sources that document the history of federal taxation are Bruce Bartlett, *The Benefit and the Burden: Tax Reform Why We Need it and What it Will Take* (New York: Simon and Schuster, 2012) and Joel Slemrod and Jon Bakija, *Taxing Ourselves: A Citizen's Guide to the Debate over Taxes 4th edition* (Cambridge, MA: MIT Press, 2008).
3. Tax Policy Center, "Alternative Minimum Tax," 2010 (http://www.taxpolicy-center.org/taxtopics/amt.cfm).
4. Congressional Budget Office, "The Distribution of Household Income and Federal Taxes," 2008 and 2009, July 10, 2012 (http://www.cbo.gov/publication/43373), 11-14.
5. Ibid, 15.
6. Chye-Ching Huang and Nathaniel Frentz, "Bush Tax Cuts Have Provided Extremely Large Benefits to Wealthiest Americans Over the Last Nine Years," Center on Budget and Policy Priorities, July 30, 2012 (http://www.cbpp.org/cms/?fa=view&id=3811).
7. Suzy Khimm, "How paying no federal income taxes helps the poor get off welfare and into work," *Washington Post*, September 18, 2012 (http://www.washingtonpost.com/blogs/ezra-klein/wp/2012/09/18/how-paying-no-federal-income-taxes-helps-the-poor-get-off-welfare-and-into-work/).
8. Thomas Piketty and Emmanuel Saez, "How Progressive is the U.S. Federal Tax System? A Historical and International Perspective," *Journal of Economic Perspectives,* Volume 21, Number 1, Winter 2007, 3-24.
9. Chuck Marr and Chye-Ching Huang, *Misconceptions and Realities About Who Pays Taxes, Center on Budget and Policy Priorities*, September 17, 2012 (http://www.cbpp.org/cms/index.cfm?fa=view&id=3505).
10. Center for Tax Justice. "Who Pays Taxes in America?" April 4, 2012 (http://ctj.org/ctjreports/2012/04/who_pays_taxes_in_america.php).
11. Patrick Fisher, *The Politics of Taxing and Spending* (Boulder, CO: Lynne Reiner, 2009), 25.
12. Suzanne Mettler, *The Submerged State: How Invisible Government Policies Undermine American Democracy* (Chicago: University of Chicago Press, 2011), pp. 20–22.
13. Congressional Budget Office, *The 2012 Long-Term Budget Outlook* (http://www.cbo.gov/publication/43288), 93–94.
14. Slemrod and Bakija, *Taxing Ourselves*, 126 & 130.
15. David Leonhardt, "Do Tax Cuts Lead to Economic Growth?" *New York Times*, September 16, 2012, SR 4.
16. Thomas L. Hungerford, "Taxes and the Economy: An Economic Analysis of the Top Tax Rates Since 1945," Congressional Research Service, September 14, 2012.
17. Slemrod and Bkija, *Taxing Ourselves*, 119.
18. Bruce Bartlett, *The Benefit and the Burden*, 45; Congressional Budget Office, The Budget and Economic Outlook 2012–2022, January 31, 2012 (http://www.cbo.gov/publication/42905), 80.

6

PREDICTING FUTURE
DEFICITS AND DEBT

Human beings yearn to know the future. Since the dawn of civilization, people have gazed into crystal balls, examined palms, dealt tarot cards, parsed the writings of Nostradamus, or the equivalent all in an effort to know what comes. So it is with debates over federal deficits and debt. We can know with certainty the pattern of U.S. fiscal history and we can measure our current fiscal state. But those concerned with deficit and debt are concerned mostly with the future. What will the country's fiscal fate be and what might we do now to control it?

Divining the future of the federal budget seems a rather straightforward exercise. In previous chapters we have looked in some detail at what goes into the current budget and how it has evolved in recent years. Why not simply extrapolate into the future what now exists and see where it takes us? This is precisely the approach of the non-partisan Congressional Budget Office (CBO), perhaps the most respected authority on budgetary matters in Washington, in its regular projections of the long-term fiscal outlook. Looking at patterns embedded in the current budget and with prudent assumptions about factors that might affect them, the CBO extrapolates into the future and predicts what the fiscal condition of the country will be over the next decades. The CBO experience with its predictions, however, raises red flags about our capacity to foresee our fiscal future. The fiscal crystal ball is fuzzy and prone to unforeseen distortions.

Take, for example, the fate of CBO's January 2001 long-term fiscal forecast.[1] This forecast was made after several years of robust economic growth in the late 1990s, producing several years of budget surplus at the end of the decade. Extrapolating from these happy circumstances

91

and projecting continuation of then-existing laws, the CBO crystal ball showed a decade of continuing surpluses of such magnitude that the entire federal debt would be paid off in 2006! By 2011, according to this rosy projection, the big problem would be, not growing national debt, but coping with accumulated surpluses amounting to $2.3 trillion. In reality, when 2011 rolled around, the federal debt had grown to an astronomical $10.4 trillion—the highest as a percentage of GDP since WWII. What happened?

The problem was not the technical expertise of CBO forecasters— had policies remained the same and the economy evolved as it seemed to be doing in 2001, their forecast would have been on the money. The problem was that things changed in unpredictable ways. Careful readers of the previous chapters already can think of what changed, but let me quickly review. First, based on this rosy scenario that suggested the government needed less revenue, Congress enacted in 2001 the Bush tax cuts, followed up by further cuts in 2003 and 2010. These cuts reduced revenues dramatically, accounting for about 21 percent of the $12 trillion shift from projected surplus to actual debt. The CBO also did not foresee 9/11 and its impact on the defense budget. The wars in Iraq and Afghanistan plus other defense increases account for 15 percent of the shift. Nor did the economy perform as robustly after 2001 as it had in the late-1990s and, most important, the CBO could not have foreseen the 2008 financial crisis and Great Recession. Sluggish growth in the 2000s and the recession alone account for about 28 percent of the shift. The stimulus spending enacted in response to the downturn added another 6 percent and other domestic spending increases unseen by CBO in 2001, including a new prescription drug benefit in Medicare, added another 12 percent to the shift. In sum, a combination of policy choices that altered dramatically the structure of revenue and spending in the budget, unforeseen events like 9/11, and poor economic performance produced a reality far different from what the best experts at CBO could predict in 2001.

So, in a chapter in which I am going to present scenarios about our fiscal future, in light of the 2001 CBO projection, I want to begin on a cautionary note about the limitations of such scenarios for predicting what the future in fact will bring. This is an especially important factor to keep in mind as I will be using CBO data, which, despite the 2001 projection, is still the most reliable information available for thinking about the fiscal future. To begin, therefore, we need to review what the CBO itself cautions about interpreting its projections.

The Fuzzy Fiscal Crystal Ball

First, any prediction about our fiscal future depends above all on future economic conditions. As we have seen, the state of the economy has a tremendous impact on the federal budget. The huge deficits incurred during the recent recession were largely a consequence of the economic downturn and only partly a result of policy choices. So it will be in the future. Rising prosperity with strong economic productivity and growth will ease efforts to reduce future debt; if growth is only sluggish, as it largely has been since 2000, then the challenge of reducing debt looms larger. If the next few decades bring more economic crises like recessions or a major financial crisis, then the fiscal future becomes very dark indeed. One argument, of course, for stabilizing deficit and debt is to allow fiscal room for responding to such crises when they occur.

While the past few years have seen low inflation rates and, most recently, low interest rates, the future might bring rising inflation and much higher interest rates. The impact of both on the budget would be huge. Moderately rising inflation could have a moderating impact on future debt. Inflation will push more taxpayers into higher tax brackets, which in turn generates higher revenues for the government. Also, inflation reduces the cost of future debt as it is paid off in dollars worth less than those that were borrowed. These, from a fiscal point of view, are the positives of inflation, but inflation also has downsides. Most economists believe that higher inflation tends to depress economic growth by reducing the future rewards from current work and investment. Although inflation might have some positive impact on future deficits, that impact will be wiped out by the negative impact inflation has on economic growth. Also, to compensate for anticipated inflation, investors demand higher interest rates, which will drive up the federal government's cost of borrowing and increase the debt. The interactions of economic growth, inflation, and budget policy are complex, largely unpredictable, and a major barrier to predictions about future deficits and debt.

Demography, the characteristics—particularly age distribution— of the population, constitutes the other class of unknowns bedeviling our ability to predict the fiscal future. We have seen how much of federal spending goes to support the incomes and health care of the elderly through Social Security, Medicare, and Medicaid and how the number of elderly recipients eligible for benefits impacts the level of spending. Extrapolating from the age distribution of the current American population, we can say with certainty that the proportion of older people in the population will grow in the future, thereby requiring increased spending on these programs. Predicting the precise number of future elderly citizens and, more importantly, the ratio of elderly entitlement recipients to workers who pay the taxes to support these programs, is more difficult to know. Yet, relatively small changes in the proportion of elderly compared to younger workers in Social Security, Medicare, and Medicaid can have large effects on spending in these programs. Most demographers anticipate that life expectancy among Americans over 65 will grow in future decades, as it has in the past, but by how much? How long will the average baby boomer now retiring live to collect her benefits? Probably the baby boomer generation will live longer than the preceding generation, but no one knows how much longer. Advances in medical science have tended to prolong life expectancy during the past century. What might be the effect of future advances on the lives of the baby boomers? What if the oft sought after "cure" for cancer were discovered in the next few years? Good news for the elderly citizens destined to get cancer, but future entitlement costs would explode as a result. (Although, depending on the nature of the cure, less cancer might reduce future health care costs.) We can know that an aging population will increase federal spending and put pressure on future debt, but knowing precisely how much is very difficult.

Estimating the number of elderly citizens is only half the budget-relevant demographic problem. The other half involves the size of the future working-age population who must provide the economic growth and tax revenue to pay for future spending. While most demographers expect the proportion of younger workers to decline compared to the elderly, the size of this decline also is quite uncertain. Much depends on future birth rates. Unlike most of Europe, Japan, and China, birth rates in the United States have declined only slightly in recent decades. If this were to change in one direction or the other, as has happened in the past, the size of the future workforce and its contribution to federal revenues would be affected. Another factor affecting the size of the workforce is immigration. Although much of the popular discourse around immigration and the budget focuses on possible budgetary costs of high levels of immigration, the larger budgetary impact of immigration is the resulting increase in the size of the workforce. Over the long run, immigration tends to increase revenues going to the government both due to positive impacts on economic growth and the taxes immigrants pay. Higher birth rates and more immigration in the future likely would reduce budget deficits, while declines in either will make the fiscal situation worse. Like with the longevity of elders, neither can be predicted with certainty.

Because of the proportion of the federal budget devoted to health care, future health costs are another huge unknown with large implications for deficits and debt. In recent decades, health costs per capita in the United States have been growing quite fast, far outpacing the per capita growth in GDP. However, in recent years, these increases have slowed somewhat, suggesting that health costs may level off in the future. The future of these costs depends on the impact of technological change, which tends to raise health care costs, and changes in the structure of the health care system, which has the potential to reduce costs. Public policy, such as the Affordable Care Act, likely will encourage efforts to make health care delivery more efficient and may affect the degree to which new technological breakthroughs affect health care costs. Because of both policy changes and changes in the health care industry, we cannot predict the future evolution of health costs. Most analysts expect health care costs to continue to rise in the future, but whether less or more rapidly than the past is unknown. This makes budgetary predictions quite difficult since what happens in this area will have great impacts on future deficits.

Finally, our fiscal future is at the mercy of war and catastrophe. Historically, the largest single factor affecting public debt around the world has been war. The impact of WWII on American debt shown in Figure 1.1 is a good example. Wars are expensive and always require public borrowing. The recent wars in Iraq and Afghanistan, for example, although relatively small engagements in terms of cost, account for about 10 percent of the growth in debt since 2000.[2] Spending on war over the next few decades will add to the national debt—how much or when, we cannot know. There are also other kinds of national emergencies that contribute to debt such as natural disasters like floods or forest fires. Inevitably, the federal government will have to spend to respond to such disasters in the future, but, again, how many and at what cost cannot be predicted. So these factors too limit our ability to accurately predict the future of deficits and debt.

Policy makers have only limited control over future economic conditions, demographic changes, rising health costs, war, and natural disasters. Policy decisions about taxing and spending, however, are factors that policy makers can control directly, and these too have a major impact on the fiscal future. But as the example of the Bush tax cuts show, predicting what policy makers will do regarding future fiscal policy choices too can be uncertain. Fiscal projections can show how alternative policy choices, which are under policy makers' control, affect future deficits and debt. Wiser policy choices—ones that moderate rather than increase future debt—make sense no matter what happens beyond policy makers' control. Fiscal projections are a tool that facilitates making these wise choices. We can look to extrapolations about the impact of alternative policy choices as a way to evaluate whether or not to adopt them.

The CBO's 2012 Budget Scenarios

In its 2012 long-term budget outlook, published in June of that year, the CBO offered a dramatic example of alternative policy choices that can lead to quite different projected budget outcomes.[3] At the time, a number of laws then in place were scheduled to produce significant policy changes at the end of 2012 that would have a major impact on future budget deficits. First the Bush tax cuts of 2001 and 2003 were scheduled to expire. Originally, these cuts were to expire at the end of 2010, but, in light of the continuing weak economy at the time, the president and Congress had agreed to extend them for two years. If the tax cuts now were allowed to expire, then the tax code would revert to what was in place prior to 2001—the same income tax rates, corporate income tax rates, capital gains rates, excise tax rates, and estate tax rates that existed under President Bill Clinton. Theses former rates would constitute a substantial tax increase, but also produce much higher levels of revenue over the long term. Second, the resolution of the confrontation of congressional Republicans and the administration over raising the debt ceiling in August of 2011 had produced the

Budget and Control Act of 2011. This legislation provided, in part, for a special committee to agree to $2 trillion in deficit reduction by November 2011 or automatic across the board cuts in discretionary spending (labeled *sequesters*) would take effect in 2013. The committee had failed to agree and the sequesters were scheduled to be imposed after the end of the year.

Finally, the so-called Medicare "doc fix" (as members of Congress refer to it) and the existing exemption on the AMT also were scheduled to expire at the end of 2012. In 1997, Congress had sought to reduce Medicare costs by mandating limits on how much physicians would be paid for their services in the program. These reductions, however, never took effect, because each year since, in response to political pressure from physicians, Congress has waived their implementation. Likewise, Congress had repeatedly raised the AMT exemption to prevent the tax from affecting additional taxpayers. If then current law were kept in place, the expiration of the doc fix would reduce physician Medicare reimbursements by about 27 percent and ensnare millions of new taxpayers in the AMT. (The media eventually would label this confluence of policy changes at the end of 2012 the "fiscal cliff.")

With the future of all these policy changes uncertain when it produced its 2012 report, the CBO had to develop two alternative scenarios in its budget projections. The first scenario, which the CBO called its "baseline" scenario, showed budget surpluses for most of the next twenty-five years which would allow a steady decline in the national debt from 73 percent of GDP in 2012 to 53 percent in 2037. If all the policies above projected to expire in current law were allowed to expire this scenario showed that if Congress and the president did nothing, then the future deficit and debt problem would be solved. The second, "alternative" fiscal scenario, which assumed that policy makers would act to continue all the expiring policies, still showed declining deficits until about 2020, then rapidly worsening ones thereafter. Under the alternative scenario, debt would rise to nearly twice the GDP in 2037—a level some would consider catastrophic.

Although made necessary by uncertainty in early 2012 about what the president and Congress would do about the scheduled expiration of these policies, the two CBO projections provided a useful exercise in clarifying what was at stake in the politics of deficit and debt. First, they showed the deficit and debt problem clearly to be more a long-term than a short-term problem. Even under the alternative fiscal scenario that assumed an extension of the all the Bush tax cuts and no spending cuts, deficits were projected to decline over the next ten years or so with the explosion in deficits occurring after the 2020s.

Second, the gap between the amounts of revenue collected under the baseline scenario and the alternative one highlighted the difference that increased revenue could make for future deficits. The alternative scenario showed that extending all tax cuts defined in the then existing policy would mean that revenue would fail to keep up with future spending. That scenario projected that as spending began to rise in about 2022, tax revenues would remain stable at about 18.5 percent of GDP through 2037. By that year, tax revenues would be about 8 percent of GDP lower than projected spending. However, if all the cuts were allowed to expire, as projected under the baseline scenario, then future deficit problems would ease substantially. Under the baseline scenario future tax revenue would exceed projected spending, excluding interest payments, far into the future. Third, the main component of future spending growth, made clear in both scenarios, is health care spending. In fact, net spending except for health care costs, according to the CBO projections, would actually decline by close to 1 percent of GDP, even factoring in a 1.2 percent increase in Social Security spending, between 2012 and 2037. What accounts for the 4 percent of GDP jump in spending? A 5 percent increase in health care spending. Controlling the spending side of future deficits and debt, both scenarios showed, primarily depends on controlling health care spending.

CBO Projects Through 2023 and Beyond

In the end, of course, policy makers adopted neither the CBO's baseline nor alternative policy scenarios; rather they crafted policies that landed in between. In the negotiations to resolve the fiscal cliff at the end of 2012 (described in detail in chapter 9), congressional Republicans and the Obama administration allowed some policies to continue but altered others. Most of the Bush tax cuts were made permanent, except for the marginal tax rates on wealthy taxpayers, which reverted to the Clinton rates; a variety of other increases targeting the wealthy such as limits on tax deductions and credits and continuation of estate taxes were included; the doc fix and AMT exemptions were reinstated, and the across the board spending cuts (the sequester) was put off for two months (but went into effect in March 2013).

Altogether policy makers enacted sufficient discretionary spending cuts and tax increases to dramatically improve the short-term budget outlook compared to CBO's alternative fiscal scenario—what would have happened if no policy changes had been made. By mid-2013, the CBO projected deficits to fall from the recession highs of 7 percent of GDP to only 3 percent on average for 2014–2023—an average similar to deficits of the previous forty years.[4] Most of this average decline was projected to occur at the beginning of the decade with deficits rising to 3.5 percent of GDP by 2023. The total debt over this period was expected to stabilize just under 75 percent of GDP during the decade, a level much higher than the 39 percent of GDP average of the four decades prior to 2008, but the rapid rise in debt during the recession would be checked. Nearly all these spending cuts had come from discretionary spending and had spared the mandatory programs that were the danger to long-term debt. While the tax increases on the wealthy would add revenue over both the short and long run, by making permanent the rest of the Bush tax cuts, revenues over the long term would be far short of what was needed to support future projected spending. After the fiscal cliff deal, CBO projections now showed an improvement in the short-term budget projections, but the long-term debt problem remained.

None of the 2012 budget changes address the long-term debt issue. The CBO's 2012 alternative fiscal scenario had projected the national debt rising to 200 percent of GDP by 2037. As most of this rise was seen as the consequence of rising health costs, the discretionary spending cuts imposed in the Budget Control Act of 2011 would be negligible in changing this scenario. The CBO's alternative scenario also assumed the continuation of the Bush tax cuts and permanent increase in the AMT exemption. With the exemption of the tax increase on the wealthy, these assumptions remain valid and projected tax revenues cannot be expected to close the long-term budget gap. Sustained levels of high future debt, these projections show, will feed on itself because of the resulting large interest payments. Without policy intervention to address rising health costs and generate additional future revenue, even the most optimistic current projections see debt rising to 400 percent of GDP by the end of the century.[5]

Many economists and budget experts would argue that the fiscal policy choices made in recent years have been the opposite of what both the economy and the fiscal stability of the country require. In the short run, the need to support economic growth in a weak economy called for continued government spending with spending restraint kicking in as the economy improved. Instead, deficit reduction will occur rapidly over the next few years while economic growth remains slow and deficits will begin to rise toward the end of the ten-year window when, presumably, the economy will be stronger. Moreover, the rapid decline in deficits probably will impede future economic growth, making the long run budget outlook worse. In addition, instead of addressing the long-term costs of mandatory spending, politicians chose to impose discretionary spending cuts—the area of the budget that funds crucial public investments, like infrastructure and education, which are needed for future economic prosperity. The imposition of premature spending cuts (and the failure to support greater stimulus spending) in the name of fiscal responsibility has, by slowing economic recovery, probably done more harm than help to our fiscal future. At the same time, the real long-term debt challenge remains unaddressed.

What Dangers Does Growing Future Debt Pose?

Projecting the future of deficits and debt, despite the uncertainties of the exercise, does offer some guidance about policy choices that need to be made now. Inexorable growth of future debt is not inevitable; prudent policy choices today can bring it under control. Among the prudent choices needed are policies to rein in future health costs. At the same time, we must be realistic about how much those costs can be restrained. Even if major innovations in health care delivery brought about lower per capita health costs, an aging population guarantees that some increase in costs are to be expected. An aging population remains a hard fact that has to be met, to some extent, through higher rates of future taxation.

The bleak scenario of the national debt rising to over twice the GDP by 2037 and continuing to rise inexorably in the years that follow is far from inevitable. Prudent fiscal policy choices over the next several years, including restraining health costs and raising more revenue, can hold future deficits at reasonable levels and keep the overall national debt in check. Given an aging population, future debt as of percentage of GDP probably will be higher through most of this century than was the norm in the past, but stabilizing it at a reasonable level would provide a sustainable long-term path.

Much commentary about America's future debt often paints overly dramatic pictures of current and future debt. Some claim that rising debt, as Republican congressman Paul Ryan did in 2011, means America is "on the brink of bankruptcy" or as Republican House Speaker John Boehner said around the same time "we're broke."[6] Others worry that future debt imposes a burden on "our grandchildren" who will be forced to pay it off.

Finally, some commentators predict the United States soon could face a fiscal crisis similar to what has occurred in Greece, Ireland, or Spain. Under this latter scenario, rising debt will produce a loss in confidence in the ability of the federal government to repay its debt leading investors to refuse to buy additional treasury bonds except at exorbitant interest rates. Without the ability to refinance the debt, the government would be forced to immediately dramatically cut spending and raise taxes, with devastating effects on the economy. How likely are any of these catastrophic scenarios?

The notion that the United States is "broke" or the government on the verge of bankruptcy greatly exaggerates our fiscal situation. The United States remains the world's richest economy and possesses tremendous assets to draw on to meet public needs. Even with the fiscal challenges we face, our $15 trillion economy, which will continue to generate wealth in the future, provides an ample cushion to meet the federal government's fiscal needs. Unlike a family in bankruptcy, a sovereign government, like the U.S. federal government, can control its income through taxation of its citizens or borrowing. Also, because federal debt is in dollars, the government, in a dire emergency, could simply devalue the currency or print more dollars to pay off debt— options unavailable to an individual. So, thinking about America's fiscal future in terms of going broke or bankrupt makes little sense. The issue is not preventing "bankruptcy" but choosing the best mix of tax and spending policies to meet public needs while maintaining future debt at levels conducive to future economic prosperity.

Nor does the idea that debt, at present or in the immediate future, imposes an unacceptable burden on "our grandchildren" make much sense as a way of thinking about deficits and debt. First, as pointed out in the first chapter, a portion of the national debt represents spending on public investments, from which future generations will benefit and for which they ought to be expected to pay. Second, even for that portion of debt resulting from "consumption" expenditures, such as Social Security payments or providing health care to aging baby boomers, these are intergenerational social insurance programs structured so that one generation supports a previous generation's consumption in exchange for a commitment of support from the next one. The financing of these programs does need to be structured and adjusted over time to make sure that the burden one generation imposes on another is sustainable; this is clearly an issue for paying the benefits of aging boomers. Some borrowing to meet the population bulge of the baby boom generation can be seen as a way of spreading the cost of this demographic event across several generations, rather than imposing all on the boomers' children. Third, if the history of the past two hundred years is our guide, we can expect future generations to be richer than the present one. Since the beginning of industrial capitalism in the nineteenth century, growing economic productivity has made each succeeding generation richer. Paying down debt gradually in the future likely will be less costly to society than imposing draconian spending cuts or astronomically high taxes at present. The most important factor preventing debt from burdening "our grandchildren" is to choose good economic policies that promote future economic growth. These include adequate levels of public investment in future growth, but also prudent fiscal policies that keep the debt itself from being too much of a drag on economic growth.

Finally, what is the prospect that the United States could become another Greece? Here the concern is that growing debt will lead to a fiscal crisis in which investors, out of concern that the debt is too high to ever be paid back, either suddenly stop lending money to the U.S. government or will do so only at exorbitant interest rates. Unable to refinance its debt at acceptable rates, the government then would be forced to cut spending drastically or raise taxes. When faced with such a situation after 2009, the Greek government faced street riots, political turmoil, and a collapsing economy. No one would like to see the United States in a similar fix.

In theory, one can imagine U.S. national debt rising to a point where it produces such a fiscal crisis. It is very difficult to predict, however, at what point U.S. debt would be so high that investors would cease to want to buy U.S. bonds. Certainly, at present, even with the rapid rise in debt over the past few years, such a fiscal crisis seems extremely unlikely to occur. For the past several years, investors worldwide have regarded owning a piece of U.S. debt the safest of investments as shown in their willingness to buy them for about zero interest (when inflation is taken into account). In a volatile world economy, the government of a powerful and rich nation like the United States is a safe bet. The fact that U.S. debt has been a safe investment for two centuries adds to investor confidence. In contrast to a small nation like Greece, debt would have to be quite high before investors would lose confidence in a large, rich nation like the United States with its history of fiscal responsibility. (Unlike Greece, which as a member of the eurozone has no control over its own currency, the United States always has options like devaluation or printing more money in the event of a crisis.)

Of course, current confidence in U.S. debt is not guaranteed to last forever. Several years of fiscal irresponsibility accompanied with continually rising debt might make investors nervous about U.S. securities. Exactly what level of debt might lead investors to do so is quite uncertain. The United States probably can experience much higher levels of debt than other countries before investor psychology would turn against its debt. Given the role of the dollar as the world's reserve currency (the one used for most international transactions), investors around the world have an economic stake in the stability of the dollar and the health of the U.S. economy. One cannot even be certain that debt rising even as high as 200 percent of GDP, as the CBO alternative scenario predicts for 2037, would cause a U.S. fiscal crisis. Depending on international conditions at that time, international investors still might regard U.S. treasuries as a safe investment. A true fiscal crisis would occur only if a prolonged period of fiscal irresponsibility, political instability, and economic decline caused governments and individual investors around the world to lose confidence in the ability of the United States to pay its future debts. The ability of U.S. political leaders, over the next few years, to devise wise taxing and spending policies, which keep deficits and debt at modest levels while sustaining economic growth, will be critical to maintain that confidence.

Notes

1. The PEW Charitable Trusts, "The Great Debt Shift," April 2011 (http://www.pewtrusts.org/uploadedFiles/wwwpewtrustsorg/Fact_Sheets/Economic_Policy/drivers_federal_debt_since_2001.pdf).
2. PEW debt report.
3. CBO, *The 2012 Long-Term Budget Outlook*, June 5, 2012 (http://www.cbo.gov/publication/43288).
4. Congressional Budget Office, *Updated Budget Projections: Fiscal Years 2013 to 2023*, May 2013 (http://www.cbo.gov/publication/44172).
5. William G. Gale and Alan J. Aurebach "Fiscal Fatigue: Tracking the Budget Outlook as Political Leaders Lurch from; One Artificial Crisis to Another," Brookings Institution Paper, February 28, 2013 (http://www.brookings.edu/research/papers/2013/02/28-fiscal-fatigue-budget-outlook-gale).
6. Richard E. Cohen, "Paul Ryan: Obama's budget means 'bankruptcy,'" *Politico*, February 14, 2011 (http://www.politico.com/news/stories/0211/49480.html).

Part II

THE POLITICS
OF DEFICITS AND DEBT

7

DEFICIT HAWKS VERSUS DEFICIT DOVES

Many of us would hope that the facts would speak for themselves, but they never do. This is as true of the facts regarding federal deficits and debt described in part I as with any set of facts. The ongoing political debate about America's fiscal future has little to do with arguments about the budgetary facts. Most participants in the debate can agree on the history of the federal taxing and spending priorities and projections of their future under different scenarios. The conflict comes over how these facts are to be interpreted and what public policy conclusions should be drawn from them.

When it comes to the federal budget, there has been an ongoing controversy for many years over how serious America's fiscal situation is. On one side are those whom I call deficit *hawks,* who paint a dire picture of our fiscal future and insist on concerted action to bring down federal deficits. The hawks claim we face a looming fiscal crisis that threatens future prosperity and the living standards of future generations. For most of the hawks, the key future threat is the large commitment to future spending in entitlement programs, particularly Medicare and Social Security. While most also argue for the need for more federal revenue to keep future debt under control, the cost of entitlements looms large in hawk rhetoric. The deficit *doves* see the worries of the hawks as overblown. The recent rise in deficits, they emphasize, is the result of the 2008 recession and, rather than a negative factor, has helped to stimulate economic revival. As the economy begins to grow over the next few years, these deficits will decline without any specific policy changes. Regarding the longer term, a wealthy nation, according to the doves, has ample resources to support entitlement commitments without serious harm to the economic well-being of future generations.

Pete Peterson's Deficit Hawk Machine

The title of Chief Deficit Hawk clearly goes to New York financier and billionaire Peter G. Peterson. A native Nebraskan and son of Greek immigrants, he began his business career in the 1950s in the advertising industry while becoming active in Republican politics. After a stint as Commerce Secretary in the Nixon administration, Peterson returned to private business rising to leadership of Lehman Brothers, the renowned New York investment bank. While still with Lehman Brothers, Peterson wrote two articles in 1982 for the *New York Review of Books* warning that Social Security was in crisis and threatened the future of the economy.[1] These articles set the stage and sounded the key themes that would inform the five books Peterson would write on the dangers of government debt. They also animated the several anti-debt organizations he would found and fund over the next thirty years.[2]

Now in his late 80s, Peterson, since he wrote those two articles on Social Security, has funded a virtual deficit and debt industry from the profits he has earned in the private equity world. Beginning in 1992, he funded the Concord Coalition led by co-chairs Democratic Senator Paul Tsongas and Republican Senator Warren Rudman. The Concord Coalition, with its bipartisan leadership and claim of a non-ideological stance, formed the pattern of all Peterson's subsequent anti-debt initiatives. The Coalition still exists today, lobbying Congress, organizing events around the country, and publishing articles spreading the deficit hawk message.[3] Most deficit hawks tend to be ideological conservatives who promote deficit reduction in tandem with their efforts to reduce the size of government. Conservative think tanks, such as the Heritage Foundation and the Cato Institute, openly connect reducing debt to the larger goal of shrinking or eliminating government programs. From the start of his foray into promoting addressing future debt, Peterson has claimed to be different from these ideologically motivated conservatives. The Concord Coalition model, with its emphasis on "moderate," "centrist," and "pragmatic" attempts to reduce debt, has been a feature of all of Peterson's efforts. However, as we shall see, deficit doves believe, despite Peterson's centrist claims, that he has helped to reinforce and advance a conservative small government agenda.

While the Concord Coalition was organizing grassroots support for the anti-debt cause, Peterson was expanding his fortune through his Blackstone Group private equity firm. In 2008, Peterson sold his stake in Blackstone for $1.8 billion and announced he would invest a large part of these gains to promoting the deficit hawk agenda. The chief vehicle for doing so now is the Peterson Foundation that funds a variety of organizations including the Committee for a Responsible Budget, an online newspaper, The Fiscal Times, and most recently, Fix the Debt, an organization of business CEOs advocating federal debt reduction.[4] Through his foundation, Peterson also provides funds to a variety of think tanks to support deficit hawk views, organizes conferences and forums on specific issues related to deficit and debt, and produces media to spread the word. In 2008, the foundation released a feature length movie, *I.O.U.S.A.*, painting a dire picture of America's fiscal future that was shown in theaters around the country and now, in both short and long versions, can be downloaded online from the foundation's web site. Peterson has used effectively the advertising skills learned in his early career to spread the deficit hawk message among both Washington policy makers and the public at large. For many, the message he has delivered for the past thirty years has become the conventional wisdom about what is amiss with American deficit and debt. So, what is that message?

The Deficit Hawk Message

The Peterson machine's over-riding message, particularly in recent years, has been to warn of the dangers of rising national debt. Yet beginning with his first articles on Social Security in the 1980s, Peterson has expressed primary concern with how future costs of entitlement programs for the elderly place the nation in fiscal jeopardy. After passage of the Bush tax cuts in 2001, the Peterson message did begin to place more emphasis on the need to raise more tax revenue as part of a "balanced approach" to reducing debt, but entitlement reform remains central to the message. Peterson's case against entitlements, consistently argued for the past thirty years, boils down to three key points. First, the New Deal promise of social insurance against life's risk was unwise and unaffordable over the long run, especially as Congress voted for more generous benefits in the 1960s and 1970s. Second, the "pay as you go" funding mechanism depends on a flawed scheme of inter-generational funding that, while successful for the first generation of entitlement recipients, will place an unsustainable burden on future generations. Finally, federal entitlements represent public consumption expenditure over public savings to the detriment of investments, public and private, in future economic prosperity.

According to Peterson, Roosevelt's "notion that government can and should 'insure' citizens against life's risks" laid the foundation for an open-ended commitment to overly generous social benefits. The system now pays workers "disabled by smoking," allows "healthy workers" to retire at age sixty-two, and pays the medical bills of "affluent Americans at age sixty-five."[5] Peterson's critique of the New Deal always has been tempered with recognition that it has laid the foundation for a crucial safety net for poor Americans. His calls for reform never attack means-tested benefits (although some deficit hawks do); rather, they target the system's generosity to those without genuine need. He attacks the "commitment to a 'social insurance scheme' under which government puts the cost of supporting affluent retirees disproportionately on the back of low-income workers."[6]

Peterson dislikes social insurance for its universality, i.e., the fact that citizens benefit from the programs irrespective of income. In light of an aging society and rising health costs, America cannot afford benefits as generous as provided through Social Security and Medicare without an "affluence test" that limits benefits for the well-off. Indiscriminate expansion of social insurance benefits, such as universal Medicare and cost of living increases in Social Security have "turned the federal government into a massive entitlement vending machine which operates by dispensing new benefits in return for organized political support and by deferring costs a as far as possible into the future."[7] The American Association for Retired Persons (AARP) features in all Peterson's books as the all-powerful special interest lobby whose advocacy for these entitlements guarantees burgeoning future debt.[8] Moreover, out of control entitlement spending threatens the entitlement programs themselves for future generations. The commitment to universal social insurance imposes an unsustainable fiscal and economic burden that will destroy these programs' ability to help those most in need of their benefits. Reform that restructures and focuses Social Security and Medicare on meeting the needs of the most vulnerable will preserve them for those who need them most.

At the core of the entitlement crisis, according to Peterson and his followers, lies their "pay-as-you-go" financing mechanism that relies on a given generation to finance the benefits of the previous generation. While inter-generational funding worked fine in supporting the benefits of the first generational cohorts in Social Security and Medicare due to the favorable ratio of workers to retirees in the past, the imminent retirements of the huge baby boom generation will fracture this financing mechanism. The aging of the population, resulting in fewer workers supporting entitlement programs combined with the generosity of entitlement benefits, amounts to "an undeclared war on our children."[9] The future generation, absent fundamental entitlement reform, will face either an unsustainable burden of financing boomer retirement benefits at the expense of their own standard of living or see the national debt rise astronomically, perhaps three times GDP by mid-century. Such a level of debt, deficit hawks warn, would destroy America's economy.

According to Peterson, had the boomer generation financed its future retirement needs "out of their own savings," then the "graying of America" would not be a problem.[10] Boomer elders would have pre-paid their retirement cost without burdening their children. Instead, Congress has enacted overly generous benefits without facing up to their ultimate cost. Inter-generational financing is seen as facilitating expanding benefits because they are provided while paying for them is pushed off on future generations. Peterson and others dramatize this situation through the calculation of the "unfunded liabilities" in entitlement programs—the value in current dollars of projected promised benefits minus projected revenues. David Walker, CEO of the Peterson Foundation, for example, claims these unfunded liabilities amounted in 2009 to $63 trillion.[11] Without substantial cut-backs in these projected benefits, these unfunded liabilities, Walker and others claim, will require imposing large tax increase in the future.

But did not the Social Security reform of 1983 impose higher payroll taxes on the boomer generation to establish a trust fund invested in Treasury securities for the purpose of pre-paying boomer retirement costs? Why has that saving not taken care of the problem? For Peterson and his allies, the trust funds contribute nothing to the fiscal health of these entitlements because they are merely IOUs that one government entity, the Treasury owes to another. In fact, this is the theme of the Peterson Foundation produced movie *I.O.U.S.A.* The film portrays the trust funds as merely parts of the overall national debt that impose obligations on future taxpayers rather than protecting Social Security and Medicare benefits. Since the Treasury will need to replace the trust funds with new debt as the funds are drawn down to pay benefits, they are not regarded as true "savings" and provide no real relief from future entitlement liabilities. Some deficit hawks even suggest that these trust fund IOUs may not even be honored when needed, forcing immediate drastic cuts in benefits.

Beyond the accounting technicalities of trust funds and unfunded liabilities, the deficit hawks make a basic moral argument against the inter-generational funding of elderly entitlements. They seem to believe that asking a younger generation to support public benefits of their elders imposes an unjust burden. If one generation has not saved sufficiently to pay all its retirement benefits, then better it experience a less comfortable retirement than demand support from the resources of the next generation. They categorically reject the notion that future economic growth will be great enough to allow future workers sufficient resources to support their elders without imposing intolerable burdens on themselves.[12] Without reductions in promised benefits, future generations will face the choice of either imposing crippling taxes on themselves or suffering from the effects of an unsustainable debt burden.

Finally, Peterson believes entitlement spending needs to be trimmed because it distorts federal policy priorities and ultimately undermines the economy. Entitlements, he argues, comprise too large a proportion of current and future federal spending, crowding out other important government investments and support for basic government services. By adding to the debt, they also increase future interest costs that further squeeze other spending. In sum, adding debt to support entitlements amounts to borrowing in order to fund societal consumption at the expense of national savings. In his earlier books in particular, he worried that public consumption on Social Security and Medicare undermined national saving needed for both private and public investment. Without those investments, future economic growth will slow.

In recent years, Peterson, while continuing to warn of future growth of entitlement spending, has included the need for additional tax revenue as a part of efforts to rein in future debt. His most recent book, *Running on Empty*, includes a detailed critique of the 2001 Bush tax cuts as ill-timed and counter-productive and he, as well as the organizations he funds, have been harshly critical of anti-tax activist Grover Norquist and those Republican politicians who signed his pledge never to raise taxes (see chapter 9). But, rather than raise revenues on higher tax rates on wealthy Americans like himself, Peterson's network tends to advocate broad tax reform that would raise revenue through reducing tax deductions and credits or through imposition of a consumption tax.[13] Peterson himself opposes elimination of the "carried interest" loophole that allows private equity managers, as he once was, to pay the lower capital gains rate on their income rather than the higher personal income rate.[14] With these caveats, Peterson's rhetoric continues to emphasize the "shared sacrifice," "compromise," and "bipartisanship" in reducing future debt. Central to the deficit hawk stance is the insistence that America's deficit and debt problems are so severe that they only can be solved through substantial sacrifice, including from the beneficiaries of Social Security and Medicare.[15]

The Deficit Doves Respond

According to deficit doves, the dire warnings of the hawks about an American fiscal crisis both exaggerate the problem and obscure the true nature of our long-term fiscal situation. Although Peterson and his allies are careful to focus the details of their analyses on future entitlement costs, their rhetoric and book and article titles tend to suggest a broader and more immediate fiscal crisis stemming from a general increase in government spending. Conservative critics of government spending seize on alarmist deficit hawk rhetoric, according to the doves, and use it to promote their agenda to reverse the New Deal and shrink the overall size of government. Despite the non-partisan and non-ideological claims of Peterson-style deficit hawks, their anti-debt campaign plays into the hands of right-wing ideologues who want to radically alter government's role in American society.

Hawkish rhetoric about deficits and debt, from the doves' perspective, obscures the complexities of America's fiscal situation. The facts do not suggest that federal spending, at present, is "out of control."[16] In fact, the General Accounting Office's December 2012 Long-Term Fiscal Outlook suggests gradual increases in elderly entitlements as baby boomers retire and, over the same period, declines in discretionary spending. And, as we saw in part I, prior to recession-induced spending starting in 2008, federal spending over several decades, well after Peterson sounded the deficit hawk alarm in the early 1980s, had remained quite stable as a proportion of GDP. If one adjusts recent deficit figures to take into account the effects of the 2008 recession, the *structural* deficit, the part of the deficit that would remain if the economy recovered, is not that high by historical standards. The structural deficit in the 1980s, for example, was much higher than the 2008–2012 deficits.[17] To the extent the structural deficit rose after 2001, it was because of tax cuts and the burst of war spending rather than any underlying massive expansion of government spending as implied in hawkish rhetoric. According to the doves, in not making careful distinctions between short-term and long-term fiscal issues and without adequate emphasis on the revenue side, deficit hawks paint a false picture of exploding government spending.

Deficit doves argue that deficit hawk alarms about the future solvency of Social Security demand special scrutiny. Beginning with his first essays in the *New York Review of Books* in the 1980s, Peterson's case for fiscal troubles in Social Security depended on lumping projected costs of Social Security, Medicare, and Medicaid together into a single "entitlement burden." Since then deficit hawks have tended to do the same whenever discussing Social Security. But, already in 1983 economist Alicia Munnell had called Peterson out on his flawed way of projecting Social Security finances.[18] Lumping projected future costs of Social Security with Medicare made both look "unsustainable" when nearly all the future increases of the combined programs derived from projected increases in Medicare due to rising health care costs. Following Munnell, many others have pointed to this flawed approach, but deficit hawks continue to cite alarmist projections of future "entitlement costs," with all programs lumped together, to justify their demands for Social Security benefit reductions in order to "save" the program.[19]

Social Security alone, deficit doves point out, has sufficient revenues from projected payroll taxes and the Social Security trust fund to comfortably pay all projected benefits for the next two decades. When the trust fund is exhausted, sometime in the 2030s, payroll tax revenues will be sufficient to cover nearly all projected benefits with only a 25 percent gap, a shortfall that needs to be addressed. As we saw in chapter 3, modest increases in program revenues, such as raising the cap on earnings subject to the Social Security tax plus other small benefit changes would assure program solvency for the long term. And, even without any policy changes and despite the supposed onslaught of baby boom retirements, projected Social Security spending will increase overall federal spending by only 1 percent of GDP two decades from now. The alarmist projections deficit hawks use of exploding entitlement costs to justify cuts in Social Security benefits collapse when Social Security finances are analyzed separate from the rising health costs in Medicare. An accurate assessment of Social Security's future, deficit doves insist, does not justify deficit hawk calls for major reductions in benefits.

Of course, this rosy view of Social Security's future depends on the reality of the trust fund which deficit hawks dismiss as merely IOUs. Deficit doves insist the trust funds to be real assets for the program and view the deficit hawks' dismissal with disdain. Treasury securities held in the Social Security trust fund, deficit doves point out, have the same legal claim to be paid as anyone's Treasury security. Failure to do so would place the U.S. government in default just as it would if the Treasury failed to redeem the bonds of individual investors or of sovereign investors such as China. Deficit hawks, such as Peterson, advocate individuals pre-paying their retirement earnings through savings during their working life but somehow dismiss the trillions workers have saved through the Social Security trust fund with extra payroll tax payments as somehow not "real." Peterson undoubtedly would regard individual purchase of Treasury bonds as a prudent component of any retirement savings plan—a secure investment in safe asset. Yet, somehow, Social Security trust fund investments in these identical Treasury securities are just IOUs. The deficit hawk trust fund skepticism makes sense only in a world where the safety of an investment asset depends not on the nature of the asset but on who happens to own it. One doubts that Peterson made that assumption during his days as a private equity investor.

Like their scary and distorted rhetoric about IOUs, the deficit hawks' calculations of huge "unfunded liabilities" in government programs needlessly alarm, according to deficit doves, without providing a realistic basis for fiscal policy making. Because entitlement programs like Social Security and Medicare are funded through a dedicated stream of payroll tax revenues, one can easily calculate the gap under current policy, the unfunded liabilities, of benefits promised to infinity over projected revenues. The future costs of government activities not funded through dedicated funding streams, like national defense, are never calculated in terms of their "unfunded liabilities" because they are not funded through such dedicated streams. If one did calculate the "unfunded liability" for national defense, in the manner deficit hawks do for entitlements, then one would produce an equally enormous sum. Calculating what money we would need to have on hand today to fund future defense needs over an infinite time horizon would be an enormous sum indeed. No one would do such a thing, however, because future defense spending will be determined by policy choices that weigh defense needs in the context of future economic capacity to support them.[20]

Likewise future spending for entitlements, whatever we can now project about "unfunded liabilities," will depend on future policy judgments about what public spending can be afforded to support the income and medical needs of retirees in the context of the overall size of the economy. Deficit hawks always make their dire projections of the "unfunded liabilities" of entitlements without putting the numbers in comparison to the GDP summed over many years. If one did so, projecting from our current GDP of $14 trillion as it will grow over future years would produce an enormous sum making even the $70–80 trillion "unfunded liabilities" claims of deficit hawks appear small in comparison. The future burden of entitlements depends not on calculations of "unfunded liabilities" today, but on the capacity of future economic growth to support future needs.

Deficit hawks come up with these alarming "unfunded liability" figures in order to convince the public to reduce public commitments to fund these future societal liabilities. Even if the deficit hawks got their wish and these unfunded liabilities were reduced through cut backs in promised benefits, the liabilities themselves, in social terms, would not go away. Reduction in promises to support income needs of future retirees in Social Security or their health care costs in Medicare would do nothing to reduce the income and medical needs of future retirees. All that would happen is the costs of these liabilities would shift from publically funded social insurance programs to the shoulders of the retirees and their children. Reducing "unfunded liabilities" in entitlement programs will not change society's costs for caring for an aging population. Such a shift, however, as deficit doves point out, would have enormous impact on how these costs will be paid and the standard of living of future retirees. The impact of entitlement cut backs would be highly unequal. Wealthier retirees could easily absorb the shift of health care costs and any reduction in Social Security income. The less wealthy would be forced to forego medical care and experience reduced living standards.

This is the heart of the disagreement between deficit hawks and doves: Deficit hawks distrust social insurance as a means of spreading the economic burden of retirement and health care broadly among all people; they prefer individuals providing for their own needs out of their individual resources. Doves, however, embrace the promise of social insurance—that vast inequality in the well-being of individuals can be mitigated if the costs of old age are widely shared. For doves, the future of Social Security and Medicare has nothing to do with calculations of "unfunded liabilities' in the programs but with "how much we're willing to spend to insure that the elderly have affordable access to health care and some financial security."[21]

"Our Grandchildren" vs. "Greedy Geezers"

Like their argument about unfunded liabilities, deficit hawk claims about "our grandchildren" being left an unsustainable debt misreads how the real economy works. According to the doves, the well-being of future generations depends much more on spurring economic growth rather than deficits and debt.[22] Rising productivity in the future would be more effective at keeping debt at sustainable levels than cutting entitlements or other government spending. In fact, the deficit hawk fixation on debt leads to counter-productive austerity policies that impede future economic growth. Misguided propaganda about "burdening our grandchildren," deficit doves say, prevented the Obama administration from enacting adequate stimulus spending to restore employment in the Great Recession. The slow recovery after 2009 and continued high employment has not only kept deficits higher than they need to be, but also contributed to slower future growth. Deficit hawk rhetoric also gets in the way of government spending on basic economic infrastructure from highways to education that provides the base for future prosperity. Moreover, cuts to entitlements in the name of "unburdening our grandchildren" will impose a double burden on future generations. First, as pointed out above, reducing social insurance benefits to the elderly does not eliminate the financial and medical needs of the elderly but only shifts the burden of those needs from entitlement programs to the elderly themselves and their children. If deficit hawks succeed in making social insurance less generous, then future generations will have to devote more of their working income to caring for their parents. Second, our future grandchildren also will lose the benefits from a social insurance system that provides adequate income and medical benefits. For doves, the deficit hawk campaign against entitlements both undermines future economic growth through unwarranted austerity and diminishes the value of future social insurance benefits. Both of these ill effects will do more to harm "our grandchildren" than will future debt.

In making their claims for entitlement belt tightening in the name of generational equity, deficit hawks often portray current entitlement recipients as "greedy geezers" living the good life at the expense of future generations. This depiction, deficit doves are quick to point out, gives a false picture of the economic situation of most of those dependent on social insurance. Most elderly Americans are not well-off geezers living their golden years in luxury. On the contrary, although Social Security serves to lift most seniors above the poverty line, the lift is not that far. In 2010, the median income for people over age sixty-five was just $25,704 for men and $15,072 for women.[23] Most elderly people depend on their Social Security checks for the bulk of their income. Deficit hawks often point to the absurdity of universal entitlement benefits going to wealthy people. In all his books, Peterson always makes the point that, despite his billions, affluent people like him get generous entitlement benefits, implying that ending such giveaways alone would reduce future debt. But entitlement payments to the relatively small proportion of wealthy Americans constitutes a miniscule part of entitlement costs. According to doves, in portraying entitlements as overly generous subsidies to those who do not really need them, deficit hawks imply benefits can be cut without substantially reducing the standard of living of most recipients. But, as deficit doves point out, benefit cuts such as reducing cost of living increases or increasing the retirement age, always on the list of deficit hawk "reforms," would reduce substantially the well-being of many elderly Americans. From a dove perspective, entitlement "reform" risks placing too much of the burden for reducing future debt on the shoulders of a population, the elderly, least able to bear it.

For most deficit doves, rather than aiding the cause of realistic policies to assure a sound fiscal future for the United States, the deficit hawk campaign against debt has promoted the impression that all government, especially entitlement spending, is leading the country to bankruptcy while obscuring the single challenge to future fiscal stability: rising health care costs. As the Congressional Budget Office (CBO) projections summarized in part I show, nearly all the long-term growth in U.S. debt derives from the rising cost of health care. If Medicare and Medicaid costs were to grow only at the rate of increase in other industrialized countries, America's future debt would be quickly stabilized. In portraying the future debt problem as one of entitlement or government spending in general, the deficit hawks create an atmosphere that leads to indiscriminate and harmful spending cuts, while deflecting attention from our real problem. Finding a way to control and finance future health care costs is at the heart of our deficit and debt problem. Rather than describe the problem accurately, deficit hawk rhetoric promotes unwarranted austerity and feeds the conservative narrative that government spending is "too big" and should be radically reduced.

An aging population and rising health costs do, even deficit doves admit, propose a long-term fiscal challenge for the United States. If current policies are unchanged, future debt, just as the hawks fear, does become unsustainable. However, reasonable policy solutions are available to mitigate future health care costs (see Chapter 10 for two alternative approaches to do so). Yet, even with effective cost reduction policies, an aging population and its health care needs will impose future costs on the public. If these costs are to be met, without bringing about unsustainable debt, future tax revenues have to be increased. Conservatives often portray the higher revenues that would be needed to pay for these future needs as impossibly high. One analysis by a conservative think tank, for example, estimates that meeting what it calls "unfunded liabilities" in future entitlement programs would require raising tax revenues from their historic average over the past fifty years of about 18 percent of GDP to 24 percent of GDP—an impossibly high figure, according to the report.[24] Yet tax revenue as a proportion of GDP in most industrial democracies around the world is much higher than 24 percent, and this level of revenue is raised without any proven harm to their economies. Reasonable controls on rising health care costs could keep the amount of taxation needed to support the health needs of the elderly lower than this 24 percent figure, but some considerable increase in tax revenue will be needed if those needs are to be met. With their focus on cutting entitlement spending as the solution, deficit hawks have down played the real need for Americans to contemplate taxing themselves more to meet future health needs. A humane society demands that elderly citizens have access to the health care they need for a decent quality of life in their final years. To provide that care through our existing social insurance system, future taxes must be raised. In the next chapter, we take up this critical part of the politics of deficit and debt: the battle over taxes.

Notes

1. Peter G. Peterson, "Social Security: The Coming Crash," New York Review of Books, December 2, 1982; "The Salvation of Social Security," *New York Review of Books*, December 16, 2012.

2. Peterson's five books: (with Neil Howe) *On Borrowed Time: How the Growth in Entitlement Spending Threatens America's Future* (San Francisco: ICS Press, 1988); *Facing Up: How to Rescue the Economy from Crushing Debt and Restore the American Dream* (New York: Simon and Schuster, 1993); *Will America Grow Up Before It Grows Old?: How the Coming Social Security Crisis Threatens You, Your Family, and Your Country* (New York: Random House, 1996); *Gray Dawn: How the Coming Age Wave Will Transform America — And the World* (New York: Random House, 1999); *Running on Empty: How the Democratic and Republican Parties Are Bankrupting Our Future and What American Can Do About It* (New York: Farrar, Straus and Giroux, 2004).

3. See the Concord Coalition at http://www.concordcoalition.org/.

4. See the Peterson Foundation at http://www.pgpf.org/; Committee for a Responsible Budget: http://crfb.org/; the Fiscal Times: http://www.thefiscaltimes.com/; Fix the Debt: http://www.fixthedebt.org/.

5. Peterson, *Running on Empty,* 110.

6. Ibid., xxvi.

7. Ibid., 18.
8. Peterson's first book, *On Borrowed Time*, claimed ARRP was America's "most powerful interest group" (72).
9. Peterson, *Running on Empty*, xxvii.
10. Ibid., 59.
11. David Walker, *Comeback America* (New York: Random House, 2010), 8.
12. Peterson, *Running on Empty*, 67.
13. Walker, *Comeback America*, 101–122.
14. Landon Thomas Jr., "Tax Break Helps a Crusader for Deficit Discipline," *New York Times,* February 15, 2008 (http://www.nytimes.com/2008/02/15/business/15pete.html?pagewanted=all&_r=0).
15. Peter G. Peterson, "How to Handle Our Long-Term Debt," *Politico*, June 27, 2012 (http://www.politico.com/news/stories/0612/77904.html).
16. Bruce Bartlett, "The Real Long-Term Budget Challenge," *Economix, New York Times*, December 11, 2012 (http://economix.blogs.nytimes.com/2012/12/11/the-real-long-term-budget-challenge/).
17. Evan Soltas, "The Deficit: Not as Bad as They Want You to Think," *Bloomberg News*, December 26, 2012 (http://www.bloomberg.com/news/2012-12-26/the-deficit-not-as-bad-as-they-want-you-to-think.html?wpisrc=nl_wonk#disqus_thread).
18. Rosemary Rinder and Alicia H. Munnell, "The Future of Social Security: An Exchange," *New York Review of Books*, March 17, 1983.
19. David Walker, *Come Back America: Turning the Country Around and Restoring Fiscal Responsibility* (New York: Random House, 2010), pp. 8-10.
20. Michael Lind, "The Right's Social Security Scare Tactics," Salon.com, May 19, 2009 (http://www.salon.com/2009/05/19/lind_3/).
21. James Surowiecki, "In Funds We Trust?" *The New Yorker*, December 24 & 31, 2012.
22. Robert Kuttner, "Greedy Geezers Reconsidered," *The American Prospect*, November/December 2012, 58.
23. Ibid, 56.
24. Liqun Liu, Andrew J. Rettenmaier, and Thomas R. Saving, "How Much Does the Government Owe?" National Center for Policy Analysis, Policy Report #338, June 2012 (http://www.ncpa.org/pdfs/st338.pdf).

8

"STARVE THE BEAST" VERSUS PROTECT THE NEW DEAL

In the introduction, we sketched the two contrasting visions in conflict over our fiscal future: one saw a smaller government essential to reducing debt, while the other did not want debt reduction at the expense of a large role for government in U.S. society. Nowhere is this divide more prominent and more partisan than in conflict over the role of tax revenues in deficit and debt reduction. The contrast results primarily from the absolute hostility of Republicans, for the past thirty years, to tax increases of any kind to address fiscal problems. Democrats have not always been enthusiastic about raising taxes and many have sometimes supported tax cuts but, in general, consider raising tax revenue a key element in addressing deficit and debt issues. Moreover, the success of the Republican Party in enacting major tax cuts and resisting their reversal has played a major role in creating the gap between government revenues and spending. Republican intransigence on the issue also has driven the gridlock of recent years over finding a bipartisan compromise on the debt. To understand the evolution of the Republican stance on taxes, we need to examine the story of "starve the beast."

Rethinking the Republican Balanced Budget Tradition

Traditionally, the core of Republican fiscal ideology and its attitude toward taxes was the party's fiscal conservatism. Until the 1980s that conservatism was defined by a strong commitment to balanced budgets even if raising taxes were required. In the early 1960s, for example, when the Kennedy administration proposed a large cut in marginal tax rates to stimulate the economy, many Republicans opposed them for fear they would drive up the deficit. This traditional Republican attitude toward balanced budgets began to change as a result of the experience with President Reagan's supply-side tax cuts. As described in chapter 5, supply-side theory claimed that large cuts in marginal tax rates could be made without increasing the deficit because the cuts would stimulate enough economic growth to make up for the cut in rates. In fact, supply-siders claimed, economic growth from marginal rate cuts would generate more revenue for the government than without them. When the supply-side impact of Reagan's tax cuts failed to materialize (in fact, revenues dropped), some conservative activists began to develop a new rationale for cutting taxes even as they retained their conviction that tax cuts promoted economic growth.

The new rationale developed out of the disappointment of many activists that Reagan proved unable to significantly reduce government spending and the size of the federal government. When Reagan, the standard bearer of the conservative wing of the Republican Party, was elected, many conservatives hoped he would undertake the conservative dream of cutting the federal government down to size, including taking on the New Deal legacy—programs like Social Security and Medicare, so dear to liberal Democrats. Although Reagan did succeed in scaling back some of the welfare state, particularly some of the expansions dating from Lyndon Johnson's Great Society of the 1960s, most federal spending was untouched or even increased.

Some of Reagan's failure to reverse the growth of government stemmed from political realities—Democrats controlled all of Congress for his entire tenure. But some resulted from conscious policy choice. Reagan was loath to cut into popular government programs, particularly middle-class entitlements like Social Security, which had the support of the "Reagan Democrats" that formed an important part of his political base. The bipartisan Social Security reform accomplished in 1983 fixed the program's long-term financing, but left the overall character of the program, and most of its benefits, intact. Moreover, Reagan found retaining big government useful to his conservative agenda when it could be used to promote conservative values. Although he had promised to abolish the Department of Education while on the campaign trail, once in office, Reagan changed his mind and used it as a vehicle to formulate a conservative agenda for America's schools. In addition, Reagan supported a massive increase in military spending to counter Soviet power. Conservative Republican activists soon realized that not only had electing a conservative president not reduced the size of government, under Reagan it had increased in size along with government spending! (They would repeat this experience under another conservative Republican, George W. Bush, in the 2000s.)

The Reagan experience convinced some Republican activists that their goal of reducing the size of government would require a long-term strategy and more than just electing Republicans to office. The rising deficits of the Reagan years also caused them to rethink the traditional Republican stance. Given his large tax cuts, Reagan could not reduce the large deficits without substantial cuts in spending. But the popularity of most government programs, particularly the most expensive entitlement programs along with the powerful interests supporting federal spending, made cutting spending a political challenge. Were deficits necessarily bad for the larger objective of recasting the role of the federal government in American life? This reflection brought about a new attitude toward both deficits and taxes that has come to be known as "starve the beast."

The Origins of "Starve the Beast"

The idea had been percolating in conservative circles for some time: the only way government spending could be cut, especially given its popularity, would be to deny the federal government the revenue needed to support the spending. Without revenue and the accompanying deficits, political pressure would build to cut spending in order to reduce deficits. As this reality actually emerged during the Reagan years, Reagan Office of Management and Budget (OMB) Director David Stockman seems to have coined the phrase "starve the beast" to describe this strategy.[1] The beast in this case was the federal government and denying it revenues was equivalent to starvation. Reagan himself made the argument saying, "Well, you know, we can lecture our children about extravagance until we run out of voice and breath. Or we can cure their extravagance by simply reducing their allowance."[2] The idea of deficits as leverage to impose spending cuts gave Republicans an added rationale for cutting taxes to the supply-side claims that tax cuts spurred economic growth. What's more, the new argument provided incentive to resist pressure to raise taxes in the face of rising deficits because the

concern over deficits themselves would put pressure on cutting spending if taxes were not on the table.

Despite its appeal, the idea of "starve the beast" initially did not take
hold. As deficits increased in the 1980s, the Reagan administration
acquiesced to small tax increases to hold them in check. At the same
time, however, a political operative named Grover Norquist, head of a
new advocacy group called Americans for Tax Reform, came up with
a new idea to stiffen the backbone of Republican politicians tempted
to agree to raise taxes. He convinced Republican members of Congress
to sign a pledge to never raise taxes—neither tax rates nor reductions
in tax deductions and tax credits. The influence of Norquist's pledge
increased enormously when, President George H.W. Bush, who had
signed the pledge, broke it by signing, in the name of deficit reduction,
a tax increase in 1990. Bush's election loss in 1992 lent credence to the
notion that breaking Norquist's pledge meant electoral defeat for any
Republican.[3] In the ensuing years signing Norquist's pledge became
required for Republican politicians. Norquist's Americans for Tax
Reform along with allied organizations, such as the libertarian Club
for Growth, enforced the pledge in Republican primaries by opposing,
and often defeating, any Republican candidate who did not sign. (As
of 2012, 238 Republican House members—an absolute majority—
and 41 Republican Senators had signed the pledge.) For two decades
after 1990, opposition to tax increases of any kind became a core prin-
ciple of the Republican Party and effectively prevented any Republican
member of Congress from voting to increase taxes. Norquist, a staunch
libertarian, views tax reduction as a critical means for radically reducing the size of the federal government until, as he has been frequently
quoted, he can "drown it in a bathtub."

The adamant Republican resistance to tax increases combined
with high deficits have been largely effective in blocking the Democratic vision of expanding the New Deal social insurance state. Since
the 1980s the Democrats have had to play defense, trying to protect
established programs, rather than expansions of social protections.
In 1993, Bill Clinton, the first Democratic president in twelve years,
found the fiscal problems inherited from the Reagan years a barrier
to a liberal agenda of expansionary government. Early in his tenure
he had to abandon planned new spending on public investments in
education and infrastructure because of deficit concerns. Instead, he

quickly shifted to an austerity agenda aimed at reducing the structural deficit, including a modest tax increase (narrowly passed without a single Republican vote) and spending restraint. Concern over limitations on increasing federal spending even shaped Clinton's failed plan to achieve the long-held liberal goal of enacting universal health insurance. Rather than the preferred liberal alternative of a single payer health system, which would have required full government financing, Clinton opted for a complex "managed competition model" that preserved the existing private health insurance system financed through employer/employee premiums.

After Republicans, under their leader Newt Gingrich, captured control of the House of Representatives in 1994, Clinton faced constant battles with Gingrich over budget issues, including a government shutdown in 1995—a prelude to the manufactured fiscal crises Obama later would face. Although Clinton "won" these confrontations with Gingrich in public opinion, achieving a decisive reelection in 1996, he had to acquiesce to Republican demands to check spending. In 1996, conservatives won the first major roll back of the New Deal legacy when Clinton signed into law a welfare reform that eliminated the welfare entitlement, replacing it with block grant funding to the states. In fiscal terms, however, the Clinton years were a great success as a booming economy, the increased revenue from his 1993 tax increase, and spending restraint eliminated the deficit. At the end of his term, the federal budget was in surplus for the first time in thirty years. "Starve the beast" may have constrained liberal expansionary policies in the 1990s, but the end of the deficit threat in 2000 opened up the prospect for a Democratic agenda of added social protections in the future.

During the 2000 presidential campaign, Republican candidate George W. Bush and Democrat Al Gore faced off over what to do with the budget surplus. Gore's position was to save projected surpluses in a "lock box" in order to shore up the finances of major entitlement programs like Social Security and Medicare. Arguing that the surpluses were the "peoples' money and ought to be returned to the people," Bush proposed an across-the-board reduction in tax rates. Bush's election decided the issue as he proceeded to enact, with some Democratic votes, a massive tax cut. Within months of their enactment, the tax cuts and a mild recession had brought back government deficits.

Increasing deficits marked Bush's tenure overall as the tax cuts reduced the flow of revenue into the Treasury and the military build-up after 9/11, including the wars in Iraq and Afghanistan, increased government spending. In addition, prior to his 2004 reelection campaign, Bush supported a new Medicare prescription drug entitlement that raised Medicare costs. Rather than consider new taxes to support any of these added expenditures, Bush added to the debt and even cut taxes further in 2003. The prevailing view within the White House seemed to be, as Vice President Dick Cheney famously said, "Reagan proved that deficits don't matter."[4]

The Impact of "Starve the Beast"

Deficits seemed not to matter as a constraint on Republican priorities such as additional tax cuts or the costs of the Iraq war, but Bush and his advisors still seemed to think that they could constrain Democratic spending priorities. Bush regarded his tax cuts as a "fiscal straitjacket for Congress" and his chief political advisor Karl Rove considered tax cut induced deficits as a strategic tool for reducing government.[5] Yet, even as "starve the beast" continued to be invoked in Republican circles, some conservatives began to question its efficacy.[6] Many were chagrined that both the Reagan and Bush administration tax cuts were followed not by spending reductions but spending increases. "Starve the beast" did not take into account how much of the spending growth of recent decades comes from mandatory spending—driven by an aging population and legal entitlements—not immediately susceptible to congressional control. Also, even Republicans have been reluctant to pay the political cost of angering the chief beneficiaries of entitlement spending—senior citizens—with major cuts in this spending. Fiscal constraints have had some impact, however, on reducing the generosity of means-tested entitlements, such as food stamps and housing subsidies, which help low-income Americans.[7] Although willing to borrow to fund middle-class entitlements, like Social Security, members of Congress consider growing deficits a compelling factor for reducing benefits to less powerful political constituents. Also, reduced government revenue in the 1980s and 1990s did seem to slow discretionary spending, particularly non-defense discretionary, as we saw in chapter 4, but it has had little impact on entitlement spending.

There also may be a partisan dynamic to "starve the beast"—as the Clinton (and later Obama) experience suggests. The deficits brought on by tax cuts may constrain Democratic administrations more than Republican ones. As the party that typically wants to expand government social protections, the Democrats must overcome the resistance of deficit hawks, even within their own party, who resist new spending programs that will add to the deficit. Starving the government of revenue does give Republicans an effective tool to resist and block Democratic attempts to expand government even if it does not prevent their own preferred spending. Whenever Democrats propose new spending, Republicans can wave the deficit flag to mobilize public and especially elite opinion against it in the name of fiscal prudence. When Republican spending priorities are at stake "deficits don't matter." For example, when Democrats pointed to rising deficits resulting from the Iraq and Afghanistan wars—suggesting that they ought to be paid for with a tax increase—the Bush administration responded that national defense had to take priority over budgetary limitations. Yet, in the final analysis, whether "starve the beast" has worked to reduce spending may be beside the point. Even if tax cuts do not reduce spending over the long term, the Republican politicians' belief that holding the line on taxes makes spending harder for Democrats and reinforces the Republican's resistance to raising taxes.

Whether or not "starve the beast" has induced lower spending, it has succeeded in lowering Americans' tax burden, as documented in chapter 5, and the amount of revenue available to support federal spending. This lower tax burden results from the trend of lower federal income tax rates since Reagan's supply-side tax cuts inaugurated the trend in 1981.[8] The most affluent tax payers have benefitted most from this declining burden—a clear payoff to those who fund the anti-tax campaigns of Grover Norquist's Americans for Tax Justice. And lower income tax rates have limited the ability of the federal government to raise tax revenue. For the decade prior to 2012, the federal individual and corporate tax revenues averaged only 9.2 percent of GDP—the lowest average for any ten-year period since WWII. By 2012, individual income tax revenues alone, which had equaled 9 percent of GDP in 1980, had shrunk to only 6.2 percent in 2010.[9] Norquist's pledge has succeeded in making resistance to taxation the new cornerstone of Republican ideology and it has had an impact on policy. To the degree that current and projected deficits are a product of too little revenue, Norquist has accomplished his goal of "starving the beast."

Revenue limits have played an important role in constraining Democratic aspirations for expanding the New Deal welfare state. Just as Clinton faced the need to pull back on increased spending programs and mold a health care reform constrained by revenue limits, the Obama administration faced similar pressures upon assuming office in 2009. Although his economic advisors warned that tax cuts would be less effective in bringing the economy out of recession than spending, tax cuts made up about one-third of Obama's 2009 stimulus package in a vain attempt to attract Republican votes for it. Like Clinton, the design of Obama's Affordable Care Act reflected the revenue constraints facing the federal government. A single-payer plan that would have drawn on general tax revenues for its financing, such as providing Medicare coverage for all Americans as some liberals advocated, was never even considered as an option. At the outset, Obama demanded that his plan could not add to the deficit, which meant limiting more generous health plans and obtaining funding through imposing reductions in Medicare costs.[10] An early proposal from House Democrats to fund the legislation through a tax on the wealthy was torpedoed by the administration still hoping to attract a few Republican votes for the legislation in the Senate. Yet, in turning to Medicare to fund Obamacare rather than from tax revenue, Obama gave the Republicans a line of attack on the program that they would use effectively through the 2012 presidential election. Even though the Medicare support would come from reduced payments to providers, rather than cuts in Medicare benefits, Republicans would accuse the administration of funding its health care reform at the expense of Medicare recipients. Obamacare opponents, ironically, used public support for one entitlement program, Medicare, to try to block the creation of another, although the use of Medicare revenues at all were a consequence of Republican adamant opposition to tapping tax revenues.

"Starve the Beast" aimed to place the federal government in a straightjacket that would finally allow conservatives to roll back the New Deal welfare state—their long-held dream. This thirty-year campaign has succeeded in reducing revenues flowing to the federal government and has lowered the federal tax burden, particularly on the rich. Reduced revenues also have been a major factor in increasing fiscal stress and raising fears of growing debt. The campaign, in particular the Norquist pledge, also has made resistance to additional tax revenue the core belief of one of America's two political parties, the Republicans. Starve the Beasters, however, still seem far from their objective.

So far, rather than shrink, the federal government has continued to grow—even with Republicans in the White House. The campaign has had some success in reducing non-defense discretionary spending and means-tested entitlements. Where it has failed has been slowing the fastest growing part of government, the social insurance entitlements that are the core of the New Deal vision. Democrats, although finding themselves often playing defense in the face of large deficits, have been resilient in keeping most of the benefits of the New Deal promise intact. Assisting them, clearly, is the popularity of the programs themselves. Although Americans claim they do not like "big government," they adore much of what it provides, particularly its most expensive parts like Social Security and Medicare. So far, "starve the beast" has done little to affect those programs. In addition, Democrats have managed to enact some expansions of the New Deal promise, in particular, adding universal health insurance, Obamacare, to the entitlement mix.

The Great Recession of 2008, however, and the deficit explosion that accompanied it gave new hope to "starve the beast" advocates. Recent deficits, also, have called attention to the projections of dire fiscal problems emerging in the next decade with aging boomer retirees and rising health care costs rapidly adding to the debt. These developments have opened a new front in the ongoing war between "starve the beast" and defend the New Deal. Advocates of reducing the size of government, with help from deficit hawks, have used the economic crisis to advance their agenda. Since Obama's election in 2008, Washington politicians have been embroiled in a constant conflict between Democrats who want to preserve the New Deal legacy and tax averse Republicans who have seized concern about future debt to promote their vision of radically reduced federal government. The conflict between these visions will be the subject of the next chapter.

Notes

1. William Grieder, "The Education of David Stockman," *Atlantic Monthly*, December 1981.
2. Quoted in David Wessel, *Red Ink: Inside the High-Stakes Politics of the Federal Budget* (New York: Crown Press, 2012), 49.
3. John Cassidy, "The Ringleader: How Grover Norquist Keeps the Conservative Movement Together," *The New Yorker*, August 1, 2005.
4. Quoted in Simon Johnson and James Kwak, *White House Burning: The Founding Fathers, Our National Debt, and Why It Matters to You* (New York: Pantheon, 2012), 69.
5. Bruce Bartlett, "The New Republican Tax Policy," *Economix, New York Times*, November 20, 2012 (http://economix.blogs.nytimes.com/2012/11/20/the-new-republican-tax-policy/).
6. William Niskanen, "Limiting Government: The Failure of Starve the Beast," *Cato Journal*, 26 (3), 2006, 553–58.
7. Marc Allen Eisner, *The American Political Economy* (New York: Routledge, 2011), 142-43.
8. Benyamin Appelbaum and Robert Gebeloff, "Complaining Aside, Most Face Lower Tax Burden Than in the Reagan '80s," *New York Times*, November 30, 2012, A-1.
9. Ibid, A-21.
10. Tom Daschle, *Getting It Done: How Obama and Congress Finally Broke the Stalemate to Make Way for Health Care Reform* (New York: St. Martin's Press, 2010), 179–82.

9

THE PARTISAN WAR OVER AMERICA'S FISCAL FUTURE

2009–2013

Among the political conflicts in which the country has been embroiled since President Obama assumed office in 2009, none has been as constant, vituperative, and partisan as the conflict over deficits and debt. Both Republicans and Democrats understand the conflict as a struggle over their core ideological commitments. For the Republicans, anxiety about the country's fiscal future calls into question the viability of the New Deal legacy of "big government" while offering a strategic opportunity to achieve their long-standing goal of bringing about a smaller federal government role in society. For Democrats, conflict over deficits and debt puts at risk their traditional commitment to a government that provides economic security, equal opportunity, and public goods to its citizens. They do not want concerns about balancing the federal government's books to place at risk an activist government needed to compensate for the inequities of the capitalist market and assure a more egalitarian society. This partisan stand-off rests at the core of budgetary politics and crises of the past few years. The widely decried budgetary gridlock in Washington stems from the parties' two contrasting visions of what America ought to be.

The Great Recession Puts Deficits on the Policy Agenda

Although the deficit hawk concern about rising federal deficits and worries about America's long-term debt outlook had been simmering for decades, the Great Recession induced spike in the federal deficit in 2009 rocketed the fiscal issue onto the political agenda. From a modest $161 billion in 2007, the deficit hit a historical high of $1.4 billion in 2009—nearly 10 percent of GDP, a post-WWII record.[1] Even though, as we saw in part I, these huge deficits had little to do with recent policy choices but were largely a consequence of the depth of the economic downturn, the size of the numbers when reported in the media raised alarm among both political elites and the wider public.

While most economists largely agreed that the immediate economic need was for a short-term increase in federal spending to stimulate the devastated economy, many politicians and pundits pointed to the rising deficits themselves as an obstacle to economic revival. Some, in contrast to Keynesian prescriptions for higher deficit spending in a recession, advocated fiscal austerity—immediate budget cuts—arguing businesses lacked confidence to invest in the American economy because of worries over rising government deficits. During the following months, fiscal turmoil in Europe, particularly the budget crisis in Greece, would fuel assertions in the media, particularly on the right, that America's fiscal situation could lead to a comparable default. Republicans made partisan use of these concerns to promote opposition to the economic stimulus plan that the Obama administration introduced soon after his inauguration. Obama even had trouble gaining support from deficit-conscious Democrats and was forced to shape his proposal to gain their votes, including both reducing its overall size and providing more tax reduction and less spending than what his economic advisors wanted.[2] Unlike economic recessions in previous decades when stimulus measures usually obtained solid bipartisan support, Obama's stimulus package passed narrowly without a single Republican vote. For their part, deficit hawks like Pete Peterson (see chapter 8), while gesturing to the need for an immediate fiscal stimulus, used the high deficits to promote their agenda for long-term budget restraint and entitlement reform.

So, even in the early months of his term, Obama came under increasing pressure to address rising deficits even as his administration sought measures to alleviate the plight of the over 10 percent of unemployed Americans. This pressure to do something about deficits only increased with the rise of the Tea Party movement.[3] During the spring and summer of 2009, groups of citizens, mostly white, conservative, and Republican, mobilized in opposition to the Obama administration and its policies. A variety of issues motivated the ire of Tea Party supporters, particularly Obama's health reform and the economic stimulus, but opposition to federal spending and the rising deficit were central concerns. In spite of its populist appearance, the Tea Party had substantial financial and logistical support from established conservative organizations, such as Freedom Works, headed by former Republican House Majority leader Dick Armey. For Armey and his allies, the Tea Party served as a vehicle to promote the long-term agenda of reducing the size of the federal government and concern about deficits was central to this strategy. Armey had long held the view that "If you're concerned about the deficit, then let me use your anxiety to cut the size of government."[4] Soon, Tea Party support would help return, in the 2010 midterm elections, a Republican majority to the House of Representatives that was committed to promoting worry over deficits as a reason to cut government, just as Armey wished.

Bowles-Simpson and the Search for a "Grand Bargain"

In the meantime, a bipartisan coalition of senators, led by Kent Conrad (D-ND) and Judd Gregg (R-NH), introduced legislation in December 2009 to create a bipartisan fiscal commission to address reducing deficits and debt.[5] This was the first of a series of efforts over the following months to forge a bipartisan "grand bargain" compromise that would set the nation on the road to long run fiscal stability. The Conrad-Gregg legislation required that the commission's recommendations receive an up or down vote in both Houses of Congress without the possibility of a filibuster. The legislation creating the commission itself *was* subject to filibuster, and a filibuster did it in.[6] A month after being introduced, even with Obama's endorsement, the bill failed to gain the sixty votes needed to overcome a filibuster going down to defeat 53-46. Tellingly the bill received bipartisan opposition with twenty-three Democrats and twenty-three Republicans voting against it, including six Republican co-sponsors who voted against an idea they had endorsed a month before. The fate of Conrad-Gregg foretold what would happen to further efforts at a grand bargain in the coming months. Although many in Congress proclaimed the need to reach a compromise on debt issues, when faced with a way to reach one, grand bargain advocates got cold feet. Republicans invariably would denounce any compromise plan because it would raise taxes (an inevitable result of any real compromise) and Democrats hesitated over likely cuts to entitlements (also a necessary component of compromise).

With Conrad-Gregg out of the picture, President Obama appointed by executive order his own commission headed by former Clinton Chief of Staff Erskine Bowles and former Republican Senator Alan Simpson. The eighteen member commission would be composed of an equal number of Republican and Democratic members of Congress, six each from the Senate and House, and six public members appointed by the president. The executive order set December 1, 2010, after the midterm elections, as the deadline for issuing a proposal and provided that if the final report received the support of fourteen members it would be introduced for vote in Congress. In early December, a report was released but received endorsement from only eleven of the commission members. All but one of the negative votes came from the congressional appointees, evenly split between Republicans and Democrats (reminiscent of Conrad-Gregg). The Bowles-Simpson report, although it fell below the threshold for automatic introduction in Congress, found strong support from many media pundits and much of the deficit hawk community. For those who demanded political action on deficits and debt, Bowles-Simpson would serve as a model for what a grand bargain might look like. As such, it would prove influential in subsequent political conflict over the budget and its proposals would shape the crafting of subsequent debt reduction plans.

Bowles-Simpson adopted a ten-year time horizon for its recommendations, in line with requirements of the congressional budget process.[7] It proposed just under $4 trillion in deficit reduction over that period which would reduce debt to 60 percent of GDP by 2023 through a balance of spending cuts and increased revenue. Deficit reduction would be achieved through caps on the growth of discretionary spending—both defense and non-defense, tax reform, and substantial cuts in mandatory spending, particularly Social Security. Discretionary spending caps would prevent increases above one-half the inflation rate and enforced through special budgetary rules requiring the Office of Management and Budget (OMB) to automatically cut spending across the board to keep spending within the caps. Congress could only stop these cuts through non-amendable votes in both the House and Senate (where it would be open to filibuster, therefore requiring sixty votes). The plan aimed to raise additional tax revenue through a tax reform involving lower tax rates in exchange for eliminating most tax expenditures. Bowles-Simpson offered three alternative versions of this approach with a top marginal rate varying between 23 and 28 percent. At the lowest rate, all tax expenditures would be eliminated; if some were kept, the tax rate would be higher to make up for the revenue loss. (This tax reform approach involving lower rates in exchange for a broader tax base through reducing tax expenditures would become a standard element in Republican deficit reduction proposals in subsequent months, although, unlike Bowles-Simpson which raised additional revenue with their proposal, the Republican plans would either keep revenues the same or reduce them.) In addition, the plan would return to taxing capital gains and dividends as ordinary income, eliminate the Alternative Minimum Tax (AMT), and reduce the corporate income tax rate (in exchange for eliminating corporate tax expenditures). All told, Bowles-Simpson sought to raise just under $1 trillion in additional revenue—about one-quarter of its projected deficit reduction. Obviously concerned that Republicans might balk at revenue increases, the plan also imposed a cap on federal tax revenues at 21 percent of GDP—3 percent higher than the 18 percent average of recent decades but one that placed an absolute limit on future tax increases. The federal government "beast," under Bowles-Simpson, would not be starved but it would be put on a diet.

Most of the mandatory spending reduction in Bowles-Simpson came from changes to the Social Security program, reflecting perhaps Senator Simpson's long-standing concern of projected increases in Social Security costs. Like the overall plan, Social Security savings came from both increased revenues and spending cuts. The plan proposed raising the maximum wages subject to the Social Security tax so that it covered a total of 90 percent of total earned income in the country which had been the case for most of the history of the program. In recent years, this percentage had gradually dropped to only 83 percent. Returning to 90 percent would mean, in real dollars, raising the taxable maximum from $106,800 in 2010 to $190,000 in 2020, generating a lot of new Social Security revenue.

Bowles-Simpson also proposed changing the Social Security Cost of Living Adjustment (COLA) by calculating on the basis of a chained Consumer Price Index (CPI) rather the traditional method of calculating inflation. Under the traditional method, CPI is based on increases in the prices of a hypothetical "market basket" of consumer goods. Some economists had long argued that this method overstated inflation because it did not take into account consumer behavior. Consumers, they argued, usually adjusted their purchases according to price increases, such as buying cheaper chicken when beef prices went up. Instead of basing cost of living on an average increase of costs across a basket of goods, the CPI should assume shifts from purchases of higher priced goods to lower priced ones, thus lowering the rate of overall cost of living. For Social Security, such a change would mean a gradual erosion of benefits as the COLA went up more gradually under a chained CPI calculation, but this also meant substantial savings. In addition to the shift to chained CPI, Bowles-Simpson reduced benefit costs by gradually increasing the retirement age from 67 to 69 by 2075. The proposal aimed to soften these benefit cuts through increases in benefits to lower income beneficiaries and the very old.

In contrast to rather specific proposals for taxes, discretionary spending, and Social Security, Bowles-Simpson, for all its subsequent reputation for "seriousness" on debt issues, was oddly vague on controlling federal health spending—the main cause of long-term deficit increases. The report only establishes a goal of capping overall growth in health care spending at the growth of GDP plus 1 percent without specifying how this will be achieved. It does endorse the cost control experiments in Obama's Affordable Care Act such as encouraging Accountable Care Organizations and payment bundling (these will be discussed in more detail in the next chapter) and the Independent Payment Advisory Board, which is supposed to recommend ways to hold the line on payments to health care providers in Medicare. While the report says that "some Commission members" believe the ACA will result in lower future health costs, if it does not keep spending growth within the cap, the report recommends "requiring both the President and Congress to make recommendations whenever average cost growth has exceeded GDP plus 1 percent." When it came to the most substantial long-term debt issue, Bowles-Simpson simply punted the problem to future political leaders.

Irrespective of the substantive value of its recommendations, the December 2010 Bowles-Simpson Commission report would be held up as the model of a bipartisan compromise for solving America's fiscal problems. Editorialists, pundits who portrayed themselves as non-partisan moderates, and politicians of both parties would urge adoption of the "sensible" Bowles-Simpson approach to deficit reduction. Mr.

Bowles and Senator Simpson went on the road, one they stayed on for the next few years, demanding action to rein in deficits and pointing to their commission's report as the way to do it. The only ones unwilling to embrace Bowles-Simpson's proposals, it seemed, were those politicians in power with the political authority to enact them. Neither Democrats nor Republicans were willing to take up the proposals because they were inconsistent with the parties' core ideological commitments. Republicans could not abide the increased tax revenue in the proposal, the reason Republican commission member, Representative Paul Ryan—soon to be House Budget Committee chairman—cited for voting against the proposal. For Democrats, the cuts to Social Security were anathema as were the cap on discretionary spending and its implication for many federal programs dear to the party. Neither party was willing to embrace the substance of Bowles-Simpson, but both were willing to use it symbolically to highlight the lack of seriousness on the budget issue by the other party's refusal to support it. Republicans especially attacked President Obama for not taking up "his" commission's proposal and pushing for its enactment. They did so even though no Republican would have voted for any proposal Obama put forward.

While neither party liked Simpson-Bowles, liberal Democrats had more reason to be wary of its specifics and how it influenced the political dynamic around the deficit issue. For all their claims to be nonpartisan and moderate, the commission's proposal leaned well to the right and, in the end, served to push the conflict over deficits in that direction. Liberals had to be unhappy that three-quarters of the deficit reduction called for in the report came from spending. Given the fundamental ideological stance of both parties, a truly middle-of-the-road plan would have sought equal savings from both spending and taxes, but Bowles-Simpson bent toward cutting the size of government. Their insistence on a long-term cap on revenues at 21 percent of GDP, in particular, served the cause of reducing the size of government. Such a cap, if deficits were to be kept in check, also acted as a spending floor. Permanently in place, a revenue cap meant future spending would have to come down even as an aging population placed additional demands on government. If revenues were subject to an arbitrary cap, then the only response to an aging population would be not meeting these needs or meeting them at the cost of other important government priorities such as education or infrastructure spending. This was "starve the beast" come true. Not surprisingly, Republicans embraced the revenue cap part of the plan, and such caps would be featured in all their budget plans over the next few years, although at levels of 18 percent or below.

Bowles and Simpson, contrary to their rhetoric of non-partisanship and moderation, also helped position the overall debate over deficits to the right. Even though they, as did their report, always insisted that their spending reductions needed to be phased in as the economy improved, their constant promotion of their report and calls for fiscal restraint created an atmosphere for immediate spending cuts. The moderate pundits who served as a sounding board for the report only served to enhance this atmosphere. After the 2010 elections, Republicans in Congress were able to take advantage of the talk of fiscal crisis, which they themselves amplified, to advance an agenda of immediate spending cuts and resistance to any attempt to stimulate a still moribund economy. The willingness of "moderates" to push the fiscal crisis atmosphere as well only built the pressure to impose immediate austerity. Not surprisingly, Pete Peterson and the deficit hawk establishment loudly embraced Bowles-Simpson and used it to promote their agenda of entitlement reduction.

Republicans Capture the House

Washington leaders at the end of 2010 could ignore Bowles-Simpson, but they could not ignore a fiscal deadline coming on December 31. This would be the first deadline of many in the ensuing months that would generate heated confrontations between the parties as they sought to take advantage of them to advance their respective agendas. The end of 2010 marked the date that the Bush tax cuts enacted in 2001 were scheduled to expire. In addition, the stimulus payroll tax cut and an extension of unemployment benefits enacted as part of Obama's 2009 stimulus were set to end. Heated negotiations ensued between the Obama administration and congressional Republicans during the lame duck period after the midterm elections to find a compromise on these issues. This face off established a pattern that would be repeated several times over the next three years, as each side adopted a position anathema to the other and held out for it until a last minute compromise was reached. In this case, the Republicans insisted on a permanent extension of the Bush tax cuts, while lukewarm to the payroll tax cut and unemployment benefit extension which the Obama administration desperately wanted given continued economic weakness. At the eleventh hour, a compromise was reached to extend for two years all the Bush tax cuts, the payroll tax cut, and extended unemployment benefits, until after the 2012 presidential election, thereby setting the deadline for what would come to be called the "fiscal cliff."

The midterm congressional elections of 2010 amounted to a victory for the Republican Party and increased Republican leverage substantially on fiscal matters. During Obama's first two years, with Democratic majorities in both the Senate and the House, the Republicans depended on the filibuster, which created the need for sixty votes to pass legislation, to advance their agenda. But success using the filibuster during this period required unity among Senate Republicans, and even united Republican support for a filibuster was of no use during the few months in 2009 when Democrats held a sixty vote filibuster-proof majority. Now a House Republican majority meant that resolving any budgetary issue would require the cooperation of the House Republican leadership. Even though Democrats retained control of the Senate, a reduced majority made any Republican filibuster threat more potent. The fact that a substantial number of victorious Republican House members had been elected under the Tea Party banner, given the Tea Party's insistence on reducing government spending, would prove especially significant in defining the dynamics of conflict with Democrats and the Obama administration over the budget.

Over the next two years and beyond, Republicans would use their new leverage to create a series of fiscal crises in which they would demand substantial spending reductions in exchange for the passage of continuing resolutions to continue funding government agencies or to increase the statutory debt limit. Because Congress had not been able to agree on a federal budget for several years, agency funding depended on periodic passage of continuing resolutions that allowed for stop-gap funding. In early 2011, House Republicans threatened not to pass such a resolution needed to continue funding through the September end of the 2011 fiscal year, which would have resulted in a government shutdown, unless federal spending were cut $61 billion.[8] Democrats and Republicans faced off over the issue for several weeks, not reaching a compromise resolution until April 8—one hour before a shutdown would begin. Republicans did not achieve their aim of a $61 billion cut but the agreement did provide for $37.8 billion of cuts, which Democrats had opposed. As the *Washington Post* put it, "An ascendant Republican Party has managed to impose its small government agenda on a town still largely controlled by Democrats."[9] This April showdown presaged a more dramatic one that would develop over raising the debt limit in August.

While they were threatening government shutdown in the name of immediate budget cuts, Republicans also used their control of the House budget process to develop their own long-term vision of America's fiscal future.[10] Reflecting the views of House Budget Committee Chairman, Congressman Paul Ryan, the budget sought to reduce the size of government eventually to 15 percent of GDP (a level not seen since the 1950s), balance the primary budget (all spending except interest payments), gradually eliminate the national debt by 2050, radically scale back entitlements, maintain defense spending levels, and reduce taxes. Ryan proposed replacing the Medicaid and Food Stamp entitlements with block grants to the states with a cap on federal commitment to these programs, as had been done in the 1996 welfare reform. The House budget even took on Medicare, the principal driver of long-term deficits, with a proposal to end the open-ended entitlement to pay the medical costs of seniors and replace it with "premium support" payments (vouchers to the plan's critics) for Medicare recipients to buy private insurance. Long-term federal budget costs were reduced substantially under this plan because the payments would be capped to grow more slowly than projected health care costs. Ryan assumed that competition among private insurers would reduce cost growth, but, if it did not, recipients would have to make up the difference between their premium support and the cost of their insurance premium. The plan sought additional savings in health care entitlement spending through repeal of the Affordable Care Act, ensuring partisan confrontation with Democrats who would never agree to gutting this recent legislative achievement in any budget deal.

The House budget plan hewed to the Republican position on taxes with proposals to reduce tax rates in exchange for reductions in tax expenditures. This "reduce tax rates but broaden the tax base" approach was similar to that in Bowles-Simpson except that the House plan was structured to reduce rather than increase future federal tax revenue. Also, like Bowles-Simpson, the plan would cap overall federal revenue but at 18 percent of GDP rather than 21 percent. Unlike Bowles-Simpson, the House budget offered no specific plans for Social Security other than a vague call for the president and Congress to agree on "common sense" reforms. Finally, to reach the targets for deficit reduction, even with substantial entitlement savings, non-defense discretionary spending would have to shrink dramatically. The House budget plan was designed to bring an end to the government commitments brought in with the New Deal. The House Republican majority passed the Committee proposal overwhelmingly as it would do with modified versions in both 2012 and 2013.

Ryan's partisan proposal received a partisan response as Democrats and the Obama administration denounced it as proposing a fiscal vision at odds with the priorities of most Americans. The Medicare voucher proposal, in particular, was widely condemned as an "end" to Medicare as Democrats looked forward to stoking fears of the Republican plan in the 2012 elections. Rather than counter the House plan with one of its own, Senate Democrats opted not to propose any budget plan at all (it would not do so until 2013). House Republicans would accuse the Democrats of ducking the "hard choices" needed to bring about fiscal stability in contrast to their own, albeit, partisan plan. Some moderate media commentators and the deficit hawk community echoed this accusation, praising Ryan for making a serious proposal in contrast to the Democrats' silence. In their defense, Senate Democrats could point to the House plan's partisan extremes which were so distant from whatever the Democrats would accept to make eventual compromise impossible. Senators also were fearful that Republicans would use any specific proposals, say to raise taxes or reduce entitlement benefits, against them in the 2012 elections. Besides, the Obama administration had released its fiscal 2012 budget which emphasized tax increases on wealthy Americans as the main approach to fiscal health and the continued need for stimulus spending given the weak economy—a Democratic alternative to what the Republicans had proposed.

The reluctance to advance specific proposals would be a constant feature of partisan jockeying over the budget through the 2012 election and beyond. Both parties were well aware of the fickle character of public opinion on issues of deficit and debt. As we saw in chapter 1, voters want politicians to reduce government spending in general, but oppose specific reductions in particular programs. Even the Ryan proposal avoided specifics in key areas such as not specifying which large cuts in non-defense discretionary spending would be made, nor did it identify which tax expenditure cuts would be needed to allow for reducing tax rates. In the spring of 2011, with the parties so far apart on how to reduce deficits and each fearful of the other exploiting the issue for electoral advantage, partisans on both sides looked to a grand bargain between Obama and the Republican congressional leadership to resolve the budget impasse. A looming fight over raising the federal debt limit would add urgency to this task and propel House Speaker John Boehner and President Obama into negotiations to find such a grand bargain.

Debt Limit Showdown

Since their resumption of control of the House, Republican leaders were under great pressure from their newly strengthened Tea Party members not to treat any future vote on raising the debt limit in a routine manner. For House Republicans, the inevitable Obama administration request to raise the debt limit by $2.4 trillion provided leverage to impose spending reductions. Their demand was for every dollar in increase in the debt limit to be matched with a dollar reduction in government spending over the subsequent ten years. Raising the debt limit did not, as we saw in part I, actually increase federal spending, it only allowed the Treasury to meet spending obligations already incurred. The Republicans still wanted to refuse allowing the House leadership to bring raising the debt limit to a vote, unless the Obama administration met its spending reduction demands. House Republicans, particularly the Tea Party faction, were oblivious to administration warnings that not raising the debt limit would result in a federal government default, rendering the Treasury unable to redeem outstanding loans or take out new ones and the requiring draconian spending cuts in all federal programs, including Social Security and Medicare. The consequence, the administration and economic experts warned, would be catastrophic for the economy and a certain return to recession.

In the face of this imminent crisis, Boehner and Obama opened negotiations in search of a grand bargain to both find a compromise on deficit reduction over the next ten years and diffuse the debt limit bomb.[11] During June and July, in advance of the August deadline for raising the debt limit, the two leaders negotiated secretly to find the elusive grand bargain framework for bipartisan agreement on debt. According to subsequent accounts, Boehner signaled willingness to allow some tax increases and Obama offered concessions on entitlements. Both agreed to cut $1.2 trillion from discretionary spending over ten years. In the end, the negotiations broke down over the amount of tax increases in the deal. Boehner later said he was willing to offer $800 billion in higher tax revenues, but Obama insisted on $1.2 trillion. Obama's defenders countered that no final tax figure had been agreed to, and Boehner withdrew because he could not sell any tax increase to House Republicans. The anti-tax pledges of many seemed to preclude many Republicans from signing on to any deal that raised tax revenue, even when agreed to by House leaders. Whatever the reason for the collapse of negotiations, a grand bargain was out of reach. Attention now turned to another round of crisis negotiations to find a stopgap to avert a debt limit crisis.

Again at the eleventh hour, one day before the debt limit would have been reached, congressional negotiators made a deal to avert federal government default.[12] The Budget Control Act of 2011 allowed an increase of the debt limit of $2.4 trillion in phases through 2013. It authorized immediate spending cuts of $917 billion over ten years but no immediate revenue increase. In addition, a congressional "super committee" made up of members from both parties from the House and Senate was to come up with an additional $1.2 billion of deficit reduction by January 2012. As incentive for an agreement, a super committee failure would result in automatic across the board spending cuts (labeled "sequesters") in discretionary spending, about equal parts defense and non-defense. The assumption was that Republican opposition to defense cuts and Democrats to non-defense would compel an agreement. Although both sides reached a stop gap agreement to prevent default, the crisis highlighted the dysfunctional, gridlocked partisanship in Washington. In the days following the debt limit agreement, Standard and Poor's, the bond rating agency, downgraded the United States rating, not for economic reasons, but because

Washington political leaders seemed unable to reach reasonable policy compromises. The obvious implication of the downgrade was that a future crisis might, in fact, lead to default.

Avoiding the Fiscal Cliff

In the end, the super committee failed to reach an agreement as Democrats insisted on some tax increases as a part of the deal and Republicans refused. The failure set in motion the automatic sequesters scheduled to take effect at the end of 2012, setting up a portion of a series of policy deadlines that would be called the "fiscal cliff." The Bush tax cuts were set to expire on that date, which would mean an automatic return to the Clinton tax rates of the 1990s. In addition, payroll tax cuts and unemployment benefit extensions enacted in Obama's stimulus were scheduled to terminate. A number of other fiscal measures also were to change including a lowering of the threshold for the AMT, potentially subjecting millions of middle-income tax payers to it, and an immediate 25 percent cut in Medicare payments to doctors. All told, this fiscal cliff would reduce the deficit dramatically—cutting it in half for 2013, but at a severe economic cost. Economists and government experts at the Congressional Budget Office predicted that going over the fiscal cliff, the automatic enactment of all these spending cuts and tax increases at once, would drive the economy once again into recession. All the drama over the debt ceiling crisis of 2011 had only set the stage for another fiscal drama scheduled to mount the stage in December 2012.

Most observers expected the outcome of the presidential election of 2012 to be the primary influence over how the 2012 fiscal cliff would be resolved. During the election campaign, Republican Mitt Romney showed his support for the fiscal vision of the House Republicans when he named the chief architect of that vision, Paul Ryan, for his running mate. Furthermore, the Romney/Ryan campaign embraced the Medicare premium support reform proposal and a version of the House tax plan for reducing tax rates in exchange for eliminating and reducing tax expenditures. As with the House plan, the campaign refused to specify which tax expenditures would go. On the other side, Obama campaigned on the need to raise taxes on the rich, proposing allowing the Bush tax cuts for those earning over $250,000 to expire and imposing a minimum tax on those earning over $1 million. Democratic candidates, including Obama, made the defense of Social Security and Medicare central to their campaigns, claiming that a Romney administration would be a threat to these programs. Romney and Ryan, however, avoided any specific proposals for Social Security and pledged that their Medicare reforms, along with their broader austerity agenda, would safeguard the retirement security of seniors. In fact, a repeated campaign accusation against Obama was that Medicare cost reductions mandated in Obamacare threatened Medicare beneficiaries even though the cuts involved reduced payments to health care providers rather than benefit cuts. These Republicans attacks on supposed Medicare cuts confirmed Democratic fears that, despite Republican calls for entitlement reform, they would not hesitate to use any Democratic proposals for such cuts against them in elections. Romney/Ryan did bemoan American's increased dependence on entitlements but referenced this word to means-tested entitlements, like Food Stamps, rather than Social Security or Medicare. Overall, the election campaign proved a showdown between the contrasting fiscal visions of the two parties, with the Republicans advocating a turn toward smaller government with less spending and lower taxes and the Democrats mounting a defense of the New Deal vision of government-provided security with taxes on the rich to pay for it.

With a re-election victory in his pocket, Obama would approach the next crisis over the fiscal cliff with renewed confidence in the Democratic vision and a determination to achieve a resolution consistent with it. He demanded that any fiscal cliff deal had to include eliminating the Bush tax cuts for those in the highest bracket while retaining the cuts for the middle class. Some Democratic strategists argued that the president's negotiating position would be stronger if the country went over the fiscal cliff, letting the Bush tax cuts expire, so that Republicans pledged not to raise taxes would be in a position to restore middle-class tax cuts after January 1. Prior to their expiration, Grover Norquist and other "starve the beasters" would place enormous pressure on Republicans not to raise taxes; afterwards, Republicans might be more amenable to letting higher taxes on the rich to remain in place in return for cutting taxes on most Americans. Obama, however, proved unwilling to adopt such a strategy fearing adverse stock market reaction to failure to reach a deal prior to January 1 and the potential harm to the economy.

As with previous crises, an agreement between Obama and congressional Republicans to avoid the fiscal cliff was not reached until the last minute. The final agreement gave Obama his objective of raising the taxes of the rich, but on those earning over $400,000 rather than $250,000. He also got Republicans to agree to extending unemployment benefits on the long-term unemployed. The payroll tax reductions did expire meaning higher taxes would be taken from the paychecks of workers. Three issues were left unresolved. Obama failed to get Republicans to agree to raise the debt limit, likely to be reached sometime in 2013, or agree to an extended continuing resolution until the end of the fiscal year in September. Both the continuing resolution and the debt limit would remain as potential Republican leverage to exact future spending reductions. In addition, the agreement did not eliminate the planned sequester, but only delayed it until March. In sum, the deal avoided the economic catastrophe that would have resulted with a fiscal cliff fall, but it did little to resolve the fiscal impasse dividing the political parties and the country. In March, the House Republicans allowed the sequester to take effect rather than respond to Obama administration pleas for a deal to avoid them, permitting the automatic spending cuts of $1.2 trillion over ten years.

After five years of partisan conflict over the budget, the prospects for a grand bargain on the model of Bowles-Simpson seemed more remote than ever in 2013.[13] Unchastened by the presidential election loss, House Budget Chairman Ryan introduced a variation on his previous proposals—one that tilted even more toward the right. The new version pushed up the date to achieve budget balance requiring even more draconian cuts in non-defense discretionary spending and means-tested entitlements. Like previous versions of the House budget, all the proposed deficit reduction came from spending cuts with no revenue increases. Unlike the previous three years, the Democratic Senate also passed its budget proposal setting up the possibility of reconciling the House and Senate versions in a conference committee according to the "regular order" of the budget process. But what Senate Democrats proposed was so distant from the House budget, the prospect of coming to a conference agreement seemed remote. Senate Democrats called for an equal amount of deficit reduction over ten years coming from spending cuts and revenue increases while offering less than one-half the total deficit reduction in the House package. In addition, the Senate plan included a short-term *increase* in deficit spending to stimulate the economy, something anathema to House Republicans. In April, President Obama introduced his own budget which included many of the elements of the failed grand bargain negotiations with Speaker Boehner in 2011. However, because his new proposal demanded additional revenue increases, Boehner denounced it as a non-starter since the president had already "got his additional tax revenue" in the December Fiscal Cliff deal. In light of the vast difference in the parties' visions of how deficits should be dealt with, any compromise seemed far out of reach.

For many political observers, the budgetary conflict not only highlighted Washington's partisan divisions, it also raised questions about the capacity of our political institutions to make sensible public policy. The Republican strategy of exploiting manufactured crises like the debt ceiling or the need to pass continuing resolutions succeeded overall in imposing their agenda of immediate austerity on the country. Their objective of reducing government also advanced, even if in a small way, as most of the short-term deficit reduction involved spending cuts rather than tax increases. But the manner in which these policy concessions were extracted alarmed many. One of America's major political parties seemed to be willing to risk economic and fiscal disaster in order to advance their ideological agenda. This mode of crisis policy making was not conducive to coming up with reasonable policy solutions to address seriously the problems of deficit and debt. Moreover, the political process after 2010 produced policies that accomplished the opposite of what most experts recommended: short-term deficit reduction while ignoring the long-term problems. The politics of deficit and debt of the past few years proved ugly and unappealing to most Americans and failed to reach the needed policy solutions.

Notes

1. Alan Blinder, *After the Music Stopped: The Financial Crisis, The Response, and The Work Ahead* (New York: Penguin Press, 2013), 387.
2. Joseph White, "From Ambition to Desperation on The Budget," ed. James Thurber, *Obama in Office* (Boulder, CO: Paradigm, 2011), 188.

3. For an accounts of the Tea Party movement see Theda Skocpol and Vanessa Williams, *The Tea Party and the Remaking of Republican Conservatism* (New York: Oxford University Press, 2012).
4. Quoted in Jacob S. Hacker and Paul Pierson, "What Krugman and Stiglitz Can Tell Us," *New York Review of Books*, September 27, 2012, 57.
5. Blinder, After the Music Stopped, 397.
6. J. Taylor Rushing, "Senate rejects deficit reduction commission," The Hill, January 26, 2010 (http://thehill.com/homenews/senate/78069-senate-rejects-fiscal-deficit-reduction-commission).
7. The Moment of Truth, Report of the National Commission on Fiscal Responsibility and Reform, December 2010, The White House, Washington, D.C. (http://www.fiscalcommission.gov/sites/fiscalcommission.gov/files/documents/TheMomentofTruth12_1_2010.pdf).
8. Paul Kane, Philip Rucker, and David A. Fahrenthold, "Government Shutdown Averted: Congress Agrees To Budget Deal, Stopgap funding," *Washington Post*, April 8, 2011 (http://www.washingtonpost.com/politics/reid-says-impasse-based-on-abortion-funding-boehner-denies-it/2011/04/08/AFO40U1C_story.html).
9. Ibid.
10. House Committee on the Budget, The Path to Prosperity: Restoring America's Promise, March 21, 2011 (http://budget.house.gov/uploadedfiles/pathtoprosperityfy2012.pdf).
11. Two detailed accounts of the Obama-Boehner negotiations are: Matt Bai, "Obama vs. Boehner: Who Killed the Debt Deal?" *New York Times Magazine*, March 28, 2012; Peter Wallsten, Lori Montgomery, and Scott Wilson, "Obama's Evolution: Behind the failed 'grand bargain' on the debt," Washington Post, March 17, 2012.
12. Jack M. Balkin, "The Not So Happy Anniversary of the Debt-Ceiling Crisis," *Atlantic Monthly,* July 31, 2012 (http://www.theatlantic.com/politics/archive/2012/07/the-not-so-happy-anniversary-of-the-debt-ceiling-crisis/260458/).
13. The following analysis of House and Senate budget proposals based on Richard Kogan, "An Apples-to Apples comparison of the Deficit-Reduction figures in the House and Senate Budget Plans," Center on Budget and Policy Priorities, March 19, 2013 (http://www.cbpp.org/cms/?fa=view&id=3933).

10

THE FUTURE OF
DEFICITS AND DEBT

As we saw in the previous chapter, while the recent politics of deficit and debt has been largely ineffectual in policy terms, it has undermined our political institutions and the public's confidence in our government. The political brinkmanship of Washington politicians risking default or haggling to the eleventh hour to avoid fiscal cliffs provided a picture of a political class caught up in its own partisan and ideological concerns at the expense of the national interest. Even if these partisan differences are rooted in sincere contrasting visions of what is good for America, as this book has argued, Republican insistence on using leverage points like the debt ceiling, in ways never used before, to advance their vision of smaller government undermines the legitimacy of the system as a whole. The fiscal threat has become then, as the Standard and Poor's downgrade said, not the federal government's actual budgetary condition, but the inability of our political institutions to allow political leaders to put in place sensible policies to stabilize the debt. Political gridlock, not economic conditions, constraints on raising tax revenue, or out of control spending, is the primary threat to future fiscal stability.

What Has the Political Controversy Over Deficits and Debt During the Last Several Years Achieved?

Deficit hawks have to be pleased about the prominence of the issue of public debt in American political discourse for the past several years. Ever since he published his initial articles in the *New York Review of Books*, Pete Peterson (see chapter 8) has wanted to set off alarm bells about the threat growing public debt posed for America's economic future. The alarms, especially in the neighborhoods of Washington's policy making elite, have been ringing loudly for some time now. The 2008 economic crisis and the resultant spike in deficits, of course, set off the alarms, but the deficit hawks had laid the ground work for debt anxiety over many years. Deficit doves would argue that the post 2008 preoccupation with deficits among the Washington elite actually deflected them from the more pressing problem of high unemployment and a sluggish economy. In their view, at a time when policy makers ought to have been focused on reviving the economy, many years of deficit hawk rhetoric made them seek premature deficit reduction instead.

While deficit hawks may have been pleased about the political conversation over these past few years, they could not be happy with its result. From the beginning, the overriding concern of Peterson and his allies has been reform of entitlement programs, particularly those like Medicare and Social Security that provide universal benefits. Yet, these programs have been spared any significant change in recent budget agreements, as the Congress and the president have produced mainly cuts in discretionary spending. In the Budget Control Act of 2011 and other negotiated cuts, Medicare and Social Security have been off the table. One argument deficit hawks often make about the need to reduce future cost of universal entitlements is that paying for them likely will come from cuts in needed discretionary spending. That argument has been born out in the various recent budget bargains. Ironically, the deficit hawks' success in fueling worries about deficits has propelled cuts precisely in places where they feel continued spending is needed and not to those programs they see as the long-term problem.

For the "starve the beast" crowd, the outcome of debt and deficit politics has been largely a success. Few Republican politicians have been willing to defy the anti-tax pledge and have become a largely unmovable obstacle against reducing deficits through revenue increases. The only exception was the increase in tax rates for the very wealthy in the December 2012 fiscal cliff agreement, which Speaker Boehner allowed to come to a vote in the House but passed with mainly Democratic votes and only a handful of Republicans. Most Republicans were able to stick to their anti-tax pledge even as this sole anti-deficit tax increase passed. Moreover, the agreement also gave Republicans a long sought victory as it made the Bush tax cuts permanent for all income below

$400,000. Overall, the record of deficit reduction measures has tilted very heavily in the direction of spending cuts rather than tax increase. The 2011 debt ceiling agreement and the 2012 fiscal cliff one produce three dollars of spending cuts for every one dollar of higher revenue.[1] Republican anti-tax fervor has become a fact assumed in all proposals and negotiations about deficit reduction. Any increases in revenue can come only if Republicans receive substantial concessions in return for deviating from their anti-tax pledge. The Republican anti-tax pledge has served as a line in the sand that allows them to demand a very high price to cross. Making raising revenue politically costly serves the "starve the beast" scenario well.

The prominence of the deficit issue on the political agenda, in fact, has served to prolong the recovery from the Great Recession. Fear of adding to the already high deficits has prevented enactment of adequate stimulus spending to reduce unemployment. Even Obama's 2009 stimulus plan, according to most accounts, was reduced to assuage congressional worries, particularly among Democrats, that it would add to the deficit. Since 2009, Federal Reserve monetary policy has been the sole tool available to stimulate economic growth even though Federal Reserve Chair Ben Bernanke has stated repeatedly the need for more fiscal stimulus to help. Although President Obama has introduced new job creating legislation, mostly in infrastructure projects, it has not received serious consideration. Of course, the deficit debate alone does not account for the failure of Obama's stimulus proposals; Republican ability to block them is the major factor. But, Republicans have had a ready excuse in the worry over deficits as a rationale to oppose all jobs legislation even in the face of continued high unemployment. In pressing for more immediate spending cuts, in exchange for raising the debt ceiling or passing a continuing resolution, Republicans have imposed an austerity regime that hurts the recovery. Cuts in public sector jobs and spending have been a major factor keeping unemployment at high levels and slowing economic growth.[2] America has avoided the profound austerity that has been imposed in much of Europe and devastated its economies, but our policies have been austere enough to cause real economic harm to too many American families.

In pure policy terms, recent deficit and debt politics have not been productive. In the main, recent budget battles have all been about reducing deficits over the next ten years and involved cuts mainly to discretionary spending. But the alarming growth in government debt is not projected to occur until the 2020s, mainly due to the rising health care costs of baby boomer seniors. Nor is discretionary spending a significant driver of future debt. Even if a "grand bargain" agreement were reached on deficit reductions to stabilize the debt for the next ten years, serious future debt problems would remain. All the disruptions and political theatre of showdowns over the debt ceiling and eleventh hour negotiations to reduce deficits have not touched on America's most significant debt problem: the long-term cost of public benefits for an aging population. Even as worry over deficits has prevented effective stimulus measures, economic growth, sluggish as it has been, has helped to relieve the budget deficit projections in the ten-year time frame. In 2013, economists at Goldman Sachs were predicting that by 2015 a growing economy would bring the deficit down from its $1 trillion high levels about to where it had been prior to the recession.[3] We have been through several years of political conflict over deficits, which may have slowed the very economic growth that will provide short-term relief, but even after these conflicts, the long-term serious debt problem remains.

What Are the Appropriate Debt and Deficit Goals for Future Budget Policy?

Some people see a balanced federal budget and even the elimination of all government debt as the goal of fiscal policy, as in the budgets Republican majorities in the House of Representatives have passed in recent years. The Republican House budget for fiscal year 2014 promises to balance the budget by 2023 and eliminate the national debt by 2050. An America with a balanced federal budget and no debt has the ring of a desirable future. As many pundits often ask: If families and state governments balance their annual budgets, why shouldn't the federal government? First, the question assumes that families and state governments always balance their budgets and seek to eliminate debt, but neither actually does. Families routinely engage in deficit spending when they take out a mortgage or a car loan. Such debts are no more problematic for families, as was argued in chapter 1, than similar long-term investments governments make with debt. State and local governments often are obligated to adopted balanced operating budgets, those that cover day to day expenses like salaries, but all have capital budgets for taking on debt for long-term projects, such as building roads, bridges, or buildings. Nearly every family, government, or business corporation in America has some debt and often has unbalanced budgets. There is no reason the federal government should be different. Making a balanced budget and debt elimination as the goals of fiscal policy ignores the positive role both debts and deficits can play, as was described in chapter 1.

Second, a positive answer to the question would ignore the significant costs bringing the federal government in balance would impose on American society and on the economy. To achieve its goal, as it also proposes more tax cuts, the House budget would require draconian cuts in valuable government spending programs across the board. As its authors make clear, its purpose goes beyond just fiscal stability, but aims to achieve the goal of a much smaller government consistent with the Republican ideological vision. In the name of fixing the problems of deficit and debt, the budget seeks a much larger ideological victory. Rapidly balancing the federal budget in the current economic circumstances would impose destructive austerity that would stifle economic growth. As pointed out above, recent spending cuts have already damaged economic recovery and further deep cuts, as would be required to balance the budget in ten years, would drag down the economy further.

The strongest argument against the goals of budget balance and ending debt altogether is that they are not needed to put the national budget on a healthy path. The goal most economists advocate for fiscal policy is debt stability, that is, debt that does not grow faster than the rate of economic growth. Even if the overall level of debt is quite high, say at the level of 75 percent of GDP as it has been in recent years or even higher, it would not be a problem if it does not continue to grow. Projections of future debt exploding after the 2020s to double or even triple the size of GDP are what should be prevented. Such a situation, most economists believe, would bring about a lower standard of living as growth stalled, interest rates rose, and interest payments ate up most government revenues. Such exploding debt can be prevented even if the federal government budget continues to have modest deficits, as long as the economy grows faster than the deficits add to the debt. As shown in Figures 1.1 and 1.2, America's huge World War II debt in relation to the economy came down rapidly during the 1950s even though the government usually ran deficits. A prudent fiscal policy should aim for modest deficits and debt stability not the extreme solutions of balanced budgets and getting rid of debt altogether.

How Can the Costs of Health Care Programs, the Biggest Factor in Long-Term Debt, Be Brought Under Control?

Everyone in the debates over deficit and debt agrees that an aging population and rising health care costs are the source of America's long-term debt problem. The deficit hawks have been right to point to how the cost of benefits to older Americans will expand enormously in coming decades. A modest and secondary component of this increase is Social Security benefits, which will rise about 1 percent of GDP by mid-century. Modest reforms in benefits and taxes, perhaps like introducing "chained CPI" or raising the ceiling on taxable wages in the Social Security tax, would cover these costs. The much bigger problem remains the projections for huge increases in government health care spending in Medicare and Medicaid. Health care cost inflation in the United States has exceeded overall inflation rates for decades. Because the elderly are generally most in need of health care, more elderly people mean more societal resources required to pay for their health care needs. The combination of an aging population and rising health care costs are why two entitlement programs, Medicare and Medicaid (which pays nearly three-fourths of its budget on the elderly in nursing homes), constitute nearly the entire rise in America's future debt. Stabilizing America's long-term debt demands finding a way to stabilize health care costs. If a solution to this problem were found, the projected exploding future debt in Congressional Budget Office (CBO) reports, congressional budget proposals, and commission plans would vanish.

Not surprisingly, embedded in recent political debate and conflict over the budget, are two contrasting approaches to reducing the federal governments future health care costs that reflect the two contrasting ideological visions of the Republicans and Democrats. The Republican approach, as Congressman Ryan has propounded in his budget proposals, would place a limit on the federal government's commitment to fund health care. Ryan wants to change Medicare from an open ended entitlement to pay the health care costs of the elderly to a system of premium support (vouchers) for recipients to buy private health insurance. Medicaid also would cease to be an entitlement that pays the health costs of all eligible recipients and become a block grant to the states to cover a portion of the costs of those each state saw fit or could afford to cover. Democrats reject both these approaches; they want to protect Medicare and Medicaid as entitlements and seek to bring down health care costs system wide. From this perspective, the budgetary costs of these programs stems not so much from the federal entitlements they embody, but the larger problem of rising costs in the nation's health care system as a whole. Addressing system wide costs will relieve the burden not only on the federal budget but also on the entire economy and society. A closer examination of these contrasting approaches will assess which would, likely, be most successful in bringing down long-term debt.

The Ryan 2014 budget, while leaving the program the same for people aged fifty-five and older, eventually would replace the existing Medicare program with a flat premium support payment that beneficiaries would use to purchase either a private health insurance plan or traditional Medicare.[4] If the plan works as envisioned, Medicare insurance exchanges set up in regions across the country (quite similar to those foreseen in Obamacare) would provide a competitive marketplace where seniors could choose from among several insurance plans, offering a range of benefits and at different costs, or traditional Medicare. The size of the premium support provided in each region would be pegged to either the cost of the second lowest cost private health insurance plan or the cost of traditional Medicare, whichever is the lowest. Seniors who choose insurance plans costing more than the premium support value would pay the difference out of pocket. The growth in Medicare spending on premium supports for new beneficiaries would be capped at a rate equivalent to the growth rate of GDP per capita plus one-half of 1 percent. For the past several decades health care costs have grown at a much faster rate than this rate cap; if they continue to do so, the value of the premium support would erode over time requiring beneficiaries to pay an increasing portion of premiums out of pocket. The CBO has estimated that, by 2050, premium supports would likely fall one-third or more short of the full cost of average insurance premiums.[5] Changing Medicare to a premium support system, then, would mean that unless the growth of health care costs dropped dramatically in future years, seniors would have to bear an increasing burden of paying for their health care costs. But this cost shift would reduce substantially the growth of the cost of Medicare to the federal government and reduce future long-term debt.

The House budget's plan for Medicare also would reduce substantially federal spending on the program. Unlike the Medicare savings from premium support which will take effect only after 2024, House Medicaid savings would kick in immediately and would reduce federal spending by nearly $4 trillion dollars by 2023.[6] The proposal to make Medicaid funding a block grant would end the federal government commitment to provide the fixed share of the total costs of eligible recipients in each state. Instead, the federal government would provide a block of funding for each state that would increase annually in accordance with the general inflation rate and the increase in the size of the U.S. population. If the federal block grant share fell short of what was needed to fund the health costs of eligible recipients, then states would have the choice of either replacing the lost federal money out of state budgets or reduce Medicaid costs by tightening eligibility requirements and thereby turning currently Medicaid eligible recipients away. Linking growth in the block grants to general inflation and population growth would assure that federal Medicaid funding increasingly would fall short of covering a state's Medicaid costs. Health care inflation historically has outpaced general inflation, and much of the cost of Medicaid goes to long-term care for the elderly—a segment of the population that will grow much faster than the general population over the next few decades.

Both the House Medicaid and Medicare plans fail to reduce future societal liabilities in these programs; instead, they shift these liabilities from the federal budget to individuals and the states. The aging population and growing health care costs that drive future federal debt would remain even as the federal government shed responsibility for covering them. The federal government's financial burden would be reduced, but the financial burden on families, individuals, and the states would grow. This burden likely would be shared unequally as wealthier and healthier seniors would easily afford adequate private insurance to cover their health needs while those with lower incomes would struggle to pay for insurance as the value of premium supports decline and less healthy seniors would find it difficult to pay for plans that address their needs. Most states would not be able to replace the declining share of federal funding resulting inevitably in more of the poor unable to access health care. Medicare premium support and Medicaid block grants, if they worked as intended, would put in place the Republican vision of an America that depends less on the federal government and relies instead on individuals, families, and local communities to meet their social needs. This vision risks, however, producing the social deprivation and inequality that the New Deal concept of social insurance entitlements was supposed to alleviate.

The shift in health liabilities described above would not impose social costs if the House reforms not only reduced federal government costs, but also slowed the increase in societal health costs. Many Republicans claim that privatizing Medicare with a system of premium supports to buy private insurance would tap the invisible hand of the market place to reduce health costs. This is supposed to happen in two ways. First, competition among private insurers will create incentives for them to negotiate lower prices with health care providers in order to be able to offer more competitive premiums. Second, insurers will offer a wider variety of insurance products including ones with substantial deductibles and co-pays in exchange for lower premiums that give health care consumers more incentive to not seek unnecessary care and be more cost conscious in their decisions regarding their own care. Experience with market competition in the existing private insurance system should make one skeptical that these cost savings will materialize. Per capita health costs in the existing employer-based and individual private insurance markets historically have grown much faster than in either Medicare or Medicaid. According to health economist Uwe Reinhardt, the fragmentation of the private health insurance system reduces the ability of individual insurance companies to negotiate lower prices with health care providers.[7] Each insurer is in competition with others to keep hospitals and doctors in their provider networks, a key factor in selling their insurance to consumers. If they pay providers too little, then health care providers will opt out of their network in favor of another insurer. If Reinhardt is correct, then moving Medicare recipients from the traditional single payer Medicare, which has the capacity to negotiate lower provider payments, to private insurers would raise health care costs, not lower them as the Ryan plan assumes.

While the Republican vision for limiting future federal liabilities for health care costs focuses on fundamental reforms in the Medicare and Medicaid entitlements, the Democrats fundamental commitment remains protecting these entitlements while addressing their future cost to the federal government through system wide health care cost control. Developing an alternative to the "fee for service" health care payment model, nearly everyone agrees, provides the key to controlling costs. While not directly mandating such a shift, the Affordable Care Act creates a framework that could encourage fundamental change through a couple of mechanisms. First, it mandates that Medicare undertake experiments with alternative payment systems to fee for service. For example, for a patient undergoing surgery, instead of paying for each step in the process separately—pre-operative visits, the cost of the surgery itself, hospital recovery, medical equipment and drugs, or any post-operative treatment—Medicare would pay a single "bundled" payment for the whole episode. Bundled payments would create incentives for the hospitals to be more efficient and work to prevent expensive post-operative complications. Another cost saving approach involves encouraging hospitals and physicians to work through Accountable Care Organizations (ACOs) that bring primary care physicians, specialists, and other health care professionals together in teams to take collective responsibility for patient care and serve as a comprehensive medical home for the patients who sign up for its care. Modeled on group practices like the Mayo or Cleveland clinics, ACO professionals are salaried and the ACO receives payment, not for each treatment of a patient, but for the overall health for each patient. ACOs would have incentives to encourage preventative care, avoid costly unneeded treatments, and assure quality outcomes. Medicare support for these and other alternatives to fee for service medicine would allow systematic assessment of their effectiveness, both in controlling costs and assuring quality care. Successful models then could be adopted throughout the health care system, perhaps with financial incentives to change from both government programs, like Medicare and Medicaid, and private health insurers.

Second, the Affordable Care Act sets up an Independent Payment Advisory Board that is supposed to monitor the growth in Medicare costs and recommend to Congress ways to reduce them if the per capita cost exceeds GDP growth plus 1 percent. Such recommendations might involve mandating shifts to more efficient payment systems based on Medicare experiments described above. Or, the federal government might use its clout as America's largest health insurer to negotiate with providers to set payment rates for various health care procedures system wide. Such rate setting negotiations are the norm in European countries that pay on average much less for comparable procedures performed in the United States.[8] (The average cost of an appendectomy, for example, in the United States runs about $13,000 while in Britain it is only $3,400, France, $4,400, and Australia, $5,400.) According to health care experts, such as Reinhardt, the United States never will get its health care costs under control unless it engages in comparable rate setting, perhaps at the state level. Only when government exerts control over the price of medical procedures will costs be held down.

The Democratic approach of looking to government led cost control contrasts sharply with the Republican one of shifting government liabilities to individuals and the states. From the perspective of the Republican vision, government promotion of bundling, ACOs, and, especially, rate setting constitute just the actions of an over-sized big government they wish to end. Yet, Democrats would respond that the security of social insurance through entitlement programs like Medicare and Medicaid cannot be abandoned in the face of rising costs. Reducing system wide health care costs, using the federal government's power to do so, will prevent rising health care costs from producing crippling debt while protecting the ability of millions of Americans to access quality health care. The gap between these two approaches to reining in health care costs reflects the broader philosophical vision of each party and mirrors the larger conflict over deficits and debt. Getting control of the national debt in the long run, however, will require finding some way to reduce rising health care costs. There is no choice between whether it will be done; the choice only is how it will be done.

Why Will Higher Levels of Taxation Be Needed to Stabilize Debt Over the Long Term?

Health care costs are the main driver of higher long-term debt, but health care cost control alone will not solve the long-term debt problem.[9] Both the Republican and Democratic approaches to health care cost control described above seek the same goal for health care cost reduction—reducing its rate of growth from 1.5 percent faster than the growth of GDP, the average of recent decades, to about .5 percent faster than GDP. Even if this goal were reached, health care spending would continue to grow and put pressure on the debt. An aging population and the inherent cost of new health care technology means additional future health spending will grow, even if the rate of increase of those costs is slowed substantially. Nor is it reasonable to expect further cuts in discretionary spending, other entitlements, or Social Security to compensate for higher health care costs. As we have seen, all spending except health care and Social Security are projected to decline over the long term as a percent of GDP, and modest reforms to Social Security can prevent it from increasing. Apart from a drastically reduced role for the federal government, greater than even most Republican ideologues would wish for, bringing the long run debt under control will demand increased future tax revenue.

As we saw in chapter 2, federal tax revenues since WWII have fluctuated between highs of just over 20 percent of GDP and lows, in the 1950s and recently between 2008 and 2010, around 15 percent, averaging for the entire period around 18 percent of GDP. Since 2001 and the enactment of the Bush tax cuts, tax revenues have been lower than this average bringing in only about 17 percent of GDP between 2002 and 2008. Tax revenues plummeted during the recession to only 15 percent of GDP, but should, according to the Tax Policy Center, climb back to around 18 percent by 2015.[10] Some argue that plans to reduce future deficits should assume raising about the same amount of tax revenue as in the past decades. The CBO, for example, projects tax revenues far into the future to stabilize at about 18 percent of GDP. The Ryan budget would allow revenues to rise above 19 percent and the Bowles-Simpson plan proposes capping revenues at 21 percent of GDP. All these projections assume that levels of tax revenue similar to what has been raised past are all that can be expected to address future debt.

This assumption may not be realistic given the aging of the population and, even with cost savings, rising health costs. These are societal burdens that we cannot escape and may require historically high levels of tax revenue, if exploding debt is to be avoided. Capping tax revenues in line with past experience simply does not take into account a new demographic reality. An older population will place added burdens of government requiring higher levels of taxation. How much revenue may be needed cannot be predicted easily, as it will depend on how much cost savings can be found in the health care system. But, Americans in the future likely will need to raise a higher percentage of federal tax revenue as a percentage of GDP than has been customary. The alternative would be either drastic cuts in all other federal spending below what would be healthy for the economy and society or an unacceptable level of debt. How might additional tax revenues be raised in the future?

One approach would be to raise additional revenue through tax reform—usually portrayed as "broadening the base" while also changing tax rates. As we have seen, in the Bowles-Simpson plan broadening the base means reducing or eliminating tax expenditures to allow some reduction in marginal tax rates. "Tax reform," however, means very different things on the different sides of the ideological divide. Republicans, as in the Ryan budget, intend tax reform to simplify the tax code, but also drastically reduce tax rates and levels of tax revenue. This approach does not expect tax reform to bring down future deficits, rather all deficit reduction is assumed to come from spending reductions. For most Democrats, tax reform is a means to raise additional tax revenue but primarily from elimination of business tax loopholes and from increased tax rates on the wealthy. Both parties, however, are reluctant to openly advocate elimination of the most popular and largest tax expenditures, such as the exclusion of medical insurance premiums and pension contributions from taxation, the mortgage interest deduction, or the charitable deductions.

Tax reform may be a way to raise future tax revenue, but it will require overcoming this partisan divide. Given the large amount of revenue which could be raised through reducing or eliminating tax expenditures, they have to be part of a revenue enhancing strategy. And, raising revenue through reform of tax expenditures need not involve eliminating popular tax breaks, but simply impose limits on how much could be deducted, targeting perhaps more affluent tax payers. For example, the mortgage interest tax deduction could be limited to a single home and applied to only mortgages up to a capped amount. A comprehensive tax reform also could limit the ability of corporations and wealthy individuals to shelter tax revenue abroad. Whenever the political circumstances lead Congress to look for ways to raise tax revenue, the amount of revenue that could be gained from tax expenditures will make tax reform an attractive option.

A second approach to raising new revenue would be the enactment of new kinds of taxes. Many tax experts believe the United States should enact a consumption tax much like the Value Added Taxes (VAT) common in Europe. These taxes are imposed, like sales taxes in most states, on the items consumers buy. Economists argue that consumption taxes help to encourage saving because the added cost of goods makes saving rather than spending more attractive. Consumption taxes also have the capacity to raise significant amounts of government revenue. Their main drawback is their regressive nature—lower income people who must spend a larger portion of their incomes on consumption pay a higher tax as a proportion of their income than do wealthier ones. Most consumption tax proposals try to get around the regressive nature of these taxes through measures that rebate portions of the tax to people with low incomes. One special kind of consumption tax, a carbon tax, also has received considerable attention recently. Carbon taxes impose a charge on the amount of fossil fuels used in the manufacture of a product. These taxes would have the greatest impact on energy purchases such as electricity and gasoline. Carbon tax advocates favor them because of their environmental effects in discouraging the use of fossil fuels, encouraging the development of alternative "clean" energy sources such as wind and solar power, and as a way of ameliorating climate change. As future Congresses and presidents look for ways to raise tax revenues in the future, these alternative forms of taxation will be on the table.

Of course, raising tax revenue to reduce future debt will face the obstacle of Republican resistance to any new taxes. As we have seen, most Republican lawmakers remain committed to the Norquist no tax pledge and their own deficit reduction proposals, like Congressman Ryan's, usually call for additional tax cuts rather than new revenue. Over the long run, however, especially when the realities of America's fiscal situation become more evident, Republican intransigence on this issue may erode. Up until now, Republicans, while embracing cutting spending in the abstract, are as reluctant to cut most specific spending programs as Democrats. In the Budget Control Act of 2011, House Republicans could support the idea of across the board spending cuts, the "sequester," which they allowed to take effect in 2013, because doing so did not name specific programs to be cut. Once the cuts began to take effect, however, Republicans were quite willing to override the sequester for programs with strong political support, as they did when furloughs of air traffic controllers delayed air travel. In the future, when faced with either profound cuts to popular entitlements, like Social Security and Medicare, or some new tax revenue, Republican politicians of the future may be more willing to look to increased revenue.

Besides, Republican opposition to raising taxes need not prevent them. In the future, there may be times when Democrats again will be in control of both Houses of Congress and the White House and not need Republican votes to raise taxes. This was the situation in 1993 when the Clinton administration raised tax rates. The Obama administration also was able to raise taxes on high income Americans as a result of the "fiscal cliff" deal in December 2012 even with Republican control of the House. Even though a vast majority of House Republicans were able to vote against the new taxes, in keeping with their no tax pledge, the fiscal cliff deal passed with mainly Democratic votes when the House leadership allowed it to come to a vote. Republicans in the future are unlikely to abandon completely their resistance to taxes, but this resistance will not always prevent raising new tax revenue anyway. Whatever the partisan balance, spending restraint alone cannot solve America's long-term debt problem and some way will have to be found to address future debt, in part, through additional tax revenue.

Will American Political Institutions Have the Capacity to Solve the Problem of Future Public Debt?

American citizens have good reason to be optimistic that solutions to our deficit and debt problem can be found. As this book has argued, we are not on the precipice of an immediate fiscal crisis. Much of the recent spike in deficits has been a result of the Great Recession. Over the next few years, as the economy recovers and with the added taxes and spending cuts enacted so far, deficits will moderate significantly. Over the next decade, there will be ample opportunity to experiment with ways to reduce health care costs, many of which are now underway. Since rising health care costs are the major factor making future debt "unsustainable," getting them under control will relieve much of the future problem. The continued strength and resilience of the American economy, despite its recent troubles, should add to citizen optimism about deficit and debt. America remains a wealthy country with a creative and dynamic population capable of generating economic growth far into the future. As a technical matter, a growing economy combined with prudent policy action could cause the prospect of ever increasing debt, which so many fear today, to melt away.

Solving our debt problem, however, as this book has argued throughout, involves much more than technical adjustments. The political conflict over deficits and debt reflects real and profound differences among American political leaders and their followers over the future direction of the country. For some time, our politics have been about the confrontation of two different visions of America's future: one that sees the federal government as a guarantor of social and economic security of its citizens through a network of social insurance protections and the other advocating an America of hardy individuals who take personal responsibility for their lives. These differences emerge in conflict over the federal budget because it embodies the value choices inherent in these contrasting visions. The tension between them shapes current budgetary conflict and likely will continue to far into the future.

So, while securing America's fiscal future does not require solving some complex policy conundrum, it does demand finding a way to bridge the gap between these two visions. Given the nature of American political institutions—the separation of powers and the ability of political minorities to veto majority proposals, neither one of these conflicting visions will be able to win a clear victory over the other, although some partisans seem to believe this possible. The intensity of recent showdowns over fiscal policy stems from this vain belief that a total partisan victory can be achieved. Until partisans set aside these dreams of total victory, sensible accommodations to resolve our fiscal problems will remain out of reach.

We probably can look forward to several more years of budgetary conflict as partisans jockey to assure a future more in keeping with their political vision. The question for our fiscal future is whether this partisan jockeying eventually can lead to the compromises needed to establish long-term fiscal stability. These compromises might not require a "grand bargain" in which value differences are bridged once and for all. A series of small incremental policy agreements in different policy areas at different points in time seems a more likely method for our political system to resolve ideological conflict. Will political leaders working through our political institutions manage to enact the prudent policy measures needed to meet our fiscal challenges? America's future fiscal stability depends on the answer to this question.

Notes

1. Richard Kiogan, "To Stabilize the Debt, Policymakers Should Seek Another $1.4 Trillion in Deficit Savings" Center on Budget and Policy Priorities, January 9, 2013 (http://www.cbpp.org/cms/?fa=view&id=3885).
2. Catherine Rampell, "Federal cuts Are Concern In Modest U.S. Growth" New York Times, Saturday, April 27, 2013, B1; Jackie Calmes and Jonthan Weisman "Emphasis on Deficit Reduction Is Seen by Economists as impeding Recovery" *New York Times* May 9, 2013, p. A19.
3. Anne Lowry, "The Incredible Shrinking Budget Deficit," *New York Times* Economix blog, April 22, 2013 (http://economix.blogs.nytimes.com/2013/04/22/the-incredible-shrinking-budget-deficit/).
4. Analysis of the Ryan budget based on Paul N. Van de Water "Medicare in Ryan's 2014 Budget," Center on Budget and Policy Priorities, March 15, 2013 (http://www.cbpp.org/cms/?fa=view&id=3922).
5. Congressional Budget Office "The Long-Term Budgetary Impact of Paths for federal Revenues and spending specified by chairman Rryan," March 2012 (http://www.cbo.gov/sites/default/files/cbofiles/attachments/03-20-Ryan_Specified_Paths_2.pdf).
6. Edwin Park and Matt Broaddus, "Ryan Block Grant Proposal Would Cut Medicaid by nearly One-Third by 2023 and More After That," Center on Budget and Policy Priorities, March 26, 2013, (http://www.cbpp.org/cms/?fa=view&id=3941).
7. Uwe E. Reinhardt "U.S. Health Care Prices Are The Elephant in the Room" *New York Times* Economix blog March 29, 2013(http://economix.blogs.nytimes.com/2013/03/29/u-s-health-care-prices-are-the-elephant-in-the-room/?pagewanted=print).
8. Ibid.
9. David Kamin "Are We There Yet? On a path to closing America's Long-Run deficit" *Tax Notes*, October 1, 2012, pp. 6–62.
10. Tax Policy Center, "Summary of Receipts, Outlays, and Surpluses or Deficits," Tax Facts (http://www.taxpolicycenter.org/taxfacts/displayafact.cfm?DocID=200&Topic2id=20&Topic3id=23).

INDEX

political conflict over deficits and debt
(*continued*): entitlements, 41–42;
public opinion on deficit and debt
debates, 1–2; Republican control of
House of Representatives, 16, 139–
43; and societal interests and values,
2–3, 26–27; taxation requirements,
160–64. *See also* "starve the beast"
strategy
presidential budget powers, 36–38
private health insurance industry, 51–52
Progressive Movement, and income tax,
73–74
progressive taxation, 81–82
progressivism. *See* liberalism
public health and non-defense
discretionary spending, 67–68
public investments in infrastructure and
education, 17–18
public opinion: and federal deficit
debate, 1–2; and federal spending
and revenue, 22, 34–35; and tax
burden, 73, 82–83
publically held debt and Treasury bonds,
10–11

R

Reagan administration, 3, 13, 18, 47, 75,
87, 123–24
recessions: deficit spending during
recessions, *12*, 15–17. *See also* Great
Recession of 2008
reconciliation bills, 38
Reinhardt, Uwe, 158, 160
Republican party: and Bowles-Simpson
report, 138–39; budget policy goals
and political conflict, 153–55;
control of House of Representatives,
16, 139–43; criticism of Obama's
economic stimulus measures, 16; and
debt limit showdown, 143–48; and
health care costs, 158–60; resistance
to emergency expenditures, 20. *See*

also "starve the beast" strategy
revenue. *See* budgets
Romney, Mitt, 145–46
Roosevelt, Franklin Delano, 3, 42, 50,
110
Rove, Karl, 127
Rudman, Warren, 108
Running on Empty (Peterson), 113
Ryan, Paul, 101, 138, 141–43, 145–46,
147, 155–56, 158

S

scientific research, non-defense
discretionary spending, 66–67
securities, U.S. Treasury bonds, 10–11
Senate Finance committee, 36
sequesters and discretionary spending,
97
Simpson, Alan, 135
social benefits and entitlements, 41–42
social democracy (liberalism), 3–5
social insurance, 42–44, 110–11
Social Security: and Bowles-Simpson
report, 136–37; deficit dove message,
113–17; deficit hawk message, 108,
109–13, 118–20; financing and
reform, 46–50; spending, 23–25, *23*,
44–45
Social Security Act, 24, 42–44
Social Security Trust Fund, 10, 46–50
societal interests and values, 2–3,
26–27
societal role of government, 2–5, 20–21,
110
spending: defense spending, 13, 23–25,
23, 62, *62*, 69–71; deficit spending
during recessions, *12*, 15–17. *See also*
budgets
"starve the beast" strategy: overview,
122, 151–52; impact of, 127–30;
origin of spending cuts strategy,
124–27; Republican fiscal
conservatism, 122–24